Nicholas,

Thank you so much for introducing me to your revolutionary ideas. It takes great courage to go against the grain of conventional wisdom and to challenge the experts. I hope that our laboratory will be able to prove the truth behind your ideas.

Congratulations and do not waiver! The truth must arise.

Professor Tim Noakes
Cape Town University

Praise for Dr. Romanov and his Pose Method

I met Dr. Romanov in 1996 at the Olympic Training Center in Colorado Springs, where he presented a workshop on the biomechanics of running. I was quite impressed by the logical simplicity of his concepts. I have since incorporated his teaching methods into the refinement of my clients' skills – and with excellent results. (I coach elite endurance athletes.) I have also relied on him for the development of a chapter on running skills in a book I'm currently writing (The Triathlete's Training Bible). His technique concepts are on the cutting edge of biomechanics and have the potential to dramatically change how running is taught.

Joe Friel, *M.S. author of Triathlete's Training Bible*
Former Chairman of USAT National Coaching Committee

Before starting Nicholas Romanov's program, I was a heel-strike runner. Nagging injuries including shin splints and upper hamstring pain plagued me. Nicholas changed my running technique based on his "Pose Method" so that I became a mid/forefoot runner. The Pose Method is the result of Nicholas' scientific study of running biomechanics in both animals and man. It allows anyone to learn the running technique, naturally used by animals and many elite runners. Along with his coordination and strength drills, this method had several beneficial effects on my running. I no longer have any pain, and I am able to train injury-free in light-weight training shoes, instead of the heavy, stiff shoes I used to require.

My running has become increasingly more efficient. It is now easy to train at a pace well below eight-minute miles, as opposed to my old 8:10-8:30 long-run pace. I now also race far more efficiently at 6:00 pace, and my track workout splits are much faster at lower heart rates.

Because Nicholas' technique allows one to use tissue elasticity as a main power source, energy-burning muscle contractions are reduced. This is especially noticeable at the start of the run portion of a triathlon. In the past, the muscle fatigue from cycling greatly hindered my running. Now, I run with minimal muscle usage, allowing me to reach my race pace much quicker and hold it for a longer time after coming off the bike.

Todd Niles Kenyon, *Ph.D.*

At the Multisport School of Champions, I worked with the Russian coach, Dr. Nicholas Romanov on my running form. After the session, I bent my knees a little bit. It looks like a shorter stride, but it's not. My leg turnover is quicker, and my foot rests on the ground less. This new running style puts less stress on my quads and back. It works, because before I was never able to do better than 1:03 for 11 miles on my tempo runs, and I managed 1:01:30 after this session. The style is more fluid; I feel 30 pounds lighter when I run.

Jurgen Zack,
5-time Europe Ironman Winner

Throughout my running career, I have been basically self-coached. During that time my training has been interrupted numerous times due to nagging injuries, feet problems, back and lower back problems. Since I've met Nicholas and have been training under his tutorage, I am becoming an injury-free athlete. Nicholas' unique exercises, flexibility and strengthening techniques have helped me tremendously. My running efficiency has improved, my overall body strength has improved; in fact, because of Nicholas' coaching, my racing times are improving; this is all happening at a time, when I am getting older, and realistically, I should be slowing down.

Nicholas has innovative flexibility, coordination, strength exercises and drills that develop one's skills. Strength exercises that deal with muscle groups, not only in the upper body and legs, but also in the lower back and hips, and abdominal area, which have never been mentioned in any of my previous running camps or clinics. These have helped me remarkably.

Mimi Oliveira, *former American Airlines flight attendant, US Track & Field Level 1 Coach, 13 marathons finisher, (Boston Marathon – 3 times)*

The Pose Method of running (developed by Dr. Romanov) has been fundamental to increasing my speed. Continually monitoring and adjusting my technique with drills and strength exercises he improves my muscle elasticity and running efficiency.

Tim Don,
2002 World Duathlon Champion, British Triathlon National Team member

The Pose method is a simple and comprehensive biomechanical model which eliminates injuries and enables every runner from novice to elite to fully utilize their physiological potential.

Graham Fletcher,
British Triathlon National Team coach

I first met Dr. Romanov two years ago after hearing about his advanced scientific training techniques from several athletes who were being coached by him in the sports of triathlon and track here in Gainesville. The athletes had so improved their performances using Dr. Romanov's sport training techniques, in such a short period of time, that they were willing to drive six hours to Miami weekly to learn and train under Dr. Romanov. I thus decided to give Dr. Romanov a try.

Over the next several months, I proceeded to meet with Dr. Romanov, both in Miami and in Gainesville, for weekly training sessions. I, as an advanced track athlete, immediately learned a new running technique developed by Dr. Romanov, and known as the "Pose Method". This technique single-handedly took tenths off my 100 meter sprint time! In addition, Dr. Romanov was instrumental in helping me overcome some debilitating injuries that had plagued me for many years.

Dr. Romanov has talents far superior than your typical coach, teacher, or personal fitness trainer. He has true expertise and vast experience in teaching and coaching, not just running technique, but the proper technique needed for world class performance in every sport imaginable (including swimming, skiing, gymnastics, cycling, etc.). That is why he has been so successful in coaching triathletes.

Dr. Romanov also knows how to structure an athlete's training program, using a specific formula he developed, to peak at the appropriate times. Additionally, he teaches proper stretching and he has a broad-based knowledge of massage and physical therapy. All of theses talents combined make Dr. Romanov an irreplaceable asset to athletes. He certainly has the potential to contribute greatly to the American sport and fitness arena.

Gene Sims, *M.S.,*
Former Ivy League Conference champion sprinter

Dr Romanov's "Pose Method of Running" is integral to our Coaching Certification program, which provides the basis for methodology used by triathlon coaches throughout the World, as it represents a biomechanically sound approach to the development of efficient, injury free running technique. The method, modeled after the mechanical properties of the wheel and the biological model demonstrated in animal running form, allows for speed development at any distance and the prevention of running injuries by using the elastic properties of the muscles involved in running. Running with a reduced chance of injury using this style will serve to conserve athletes' energy and prolong their competitive career in the sport.

George M. Dallam, Ph.D.
Assistant Professor, Dept. of Exercise Science,
Univ. of Southern Colorado
Former USAT National Team Head Coach

I came to Nicholas as a discouraged competitive runner and triathlete, disappointed over the years by a litany of injuries. I'd achieved relative success locally and nationally, but was getting injured more and more frequently. I was seeking advice, but did not hold out much hope as all the experts I'd consulted in the past: doctors, physical therapists, running coaches, chiropractors, and running publications had not been any help at all. Not only did Nicholas have solutions for curing what had become a chronic injury, but he has introduced me to a new brand of training, and an approach to movement that has virtually eliminated the potential for injury, and brought me to a state of balance from which I have been able to develop unprecedented levels of strength, power and speed.
Nicholas' human qualities and unique theories distinguish him as unequaled mentor and effective coach. Other trainers draw runners and simply provide them with workouts, but Nicholas is the only one who is teaching people to run or do their sport correctly. He alone has the knowledge about biomechanics to break down the movements and help athletes to work as efficiently and powerfully as possible. Nicholas teaches a whole philosophy that the athlete continues to grow and improve with. His pedagogic skills, thorough knowledge, and giving nature combine to distinguish Nicholas as a uniquely qualified coach.

Lynn McFadden,
Top South Florida triathlete

Dr. Romanov's "Pose Method" is the preferred method for teaching running technique for the Triathlon Coaches Certification program and manual. Dr. Romanov's unique approach to training based on applied scientific theory and incorporating biomechanical movement theory into the development of speed and strength is not commonly found amongst US coaches. These unique methods have reduced the incidence of injury and enhanced the performance of many National Team members.

Cyle Sage,
Former USAT Development Director
National Team Coach

For the past several years I was continuously incurring injuries from running. I was never able to run for more than two months before an injury would occur. In addition I had a "bad back" that would "go out" every 6 to 8 weeks. For my "bad back" doctors and physical therapists could do no more than give the standard advice, stretch and exercise. Their stretches and exercises were useless.

On a recommendation from a friend, I sought help from Nicholas. My back is now much much better.He has improved my running technique so that I now run practically injury free. He has given me unique exercises that have enabled me to develop all the muscle groups in my body.

Nicholas has unique knowledge of exercises, stretches, and running techniques that no doctors, physical therapists, coaches, or books I have encountered come close to matching. Beyond his knowledge, he has a tremendous ability to analyze physical problems and come up with solutions.

Roy Siegel, *M.S.,*
computer systems analyst

I have started your Pose Method of running and its training. I can definitely see the efficiency of this running method. My normal weekly distance is 18-25 miles a week. I am 48 years old, and am 6'3 and weigh 210. I have had injuries in the past, but have recovered nicely. I feel this new method is my way to improve and enable me to run into the later years of my life. I enjoy Duathlon events and plan to do my second half iron man event this summer.

Michael Ruedisyeli,
Lambertville, MI

After Dr. Romanov's lecture I was very excited. I bought his video, took it home and watched it that night. The next day, at the race, I tried it out. Immediately, the pains I had been feeling in my hips, knees, and back were gone. Where is the pain? Surely it would be back by the next mile? It never came back, I was hooked. Now, my first attempt at running with Pose technique was crude, and my calve muscles were in knots by the end of the race (due to pushing off, and not relaxing the ankles). It takes more than a quick glance at the video, to correct 30 years of Poor Running technique.

It's not just about technique, Dr. Romanov has developed an entirely new revolutionary way to train. A method that doesn't beat runners into the ground, trying to make them tough, but instead, "adapts" the body and mind to faster and faster speed and endurance. "Adaptation" is the key. He makes heavy use of heart rate monitors and recovery times, so you never use any of your future energy credits, except, of course, on race day.

Open any running magazine, and it's mostly discussion of running injuries, ads and reviews for the latest padded shoes, and different injury treatments. People are trying to bring joy, and improve their lives, through running. They are confused when they are rewarded with debilitating injury. Even the best elite runners in the world are in constant fear of injury! Is this fair? Is this necessary? Of course not!

With the Pose method the risk of injury is virtually nill, and your times improve quickly and steadily. I wanted to help Dr. Romanov get the information out, and to try to introduce a new paradigm of running to the world. Sounds like fun. Wish us luck! Change the way you run, then spread the word!

Stefan Hunter,
Key West, FL

I have been running up to 40 miles a week. No pain, no nothing. My shoes wear out a little in the back, but the ball of my shoe is fine. So I just wanted to drop you a line to tell you that I actually did learn something after all those lessons. I am injury free and taking real advantage of it.

Lawrence Lee,
Miami, FL

ISBN 0-9725537-6-2

For Information, contact: PoseTech Corp.,
1211 Venetia Avenue, Coral Gables, FL 33134,
Or e-mail: Info@PoseTech.com

For Info about PoseTech clinics, call 877-POSE-TEC
or visit our website at: www.PoseTech.com.

Text and Concept: Nicholas Romanov, Ph.D. with John Robson
Editing: Svetlana Romanov, Ph.D.
Cover Photo & Design: SunnyWorld Productions
Photography: Lana Romanov
Illustrations: Andrew Pianzin, Ph. D. & Sylvia Corbett
Book Design: Severin & Marianna Romanov

Published by PoseTech Press

Library of Congress Catalog Number 2004091106

Printed in the United States of America

To my grandmother, Maria, my dear Santa Maria, whose affection and kindness I'll always cherish and remember.

To my beloved first-born daughter, Marianna, who wanted us to reach the stars, but left us so unexpectedly early.

To my wife, Svetlana, whose love and faith in me have always guided me through this journey, called Life, and whose constant support has helped me realize my dreams, this book always being the best of them.

CONTENTS

Section Five: Building A Runner's Body…And Mind

Section Six: Refining Your Running Technique

ACKNOWLEDGEMENTS

It is almost impossible to mention everyone to whom I would like to express my gratitude for helping me to bring the Pose Method of Running to you, my reader. Nevertheless, I want to mention those without whom this book would never have made it to print.

To my family (AKA Team Romanov) for their unconditional love and uncompromised dedication to my ideas throughout my life. To my wife, Svetlana, whose masterful translation, helped me express these ideas to the world.

To my co-author and friend, John Robson, whose brilliant writing talent made those ideas an easy and enjoyable reading. To my students and friends, Dr. Andrey Pianzin (Russia) and Sylvia Corbet (Canada), for their beautiful illustrations, which made my ideas visual.

To Milton Ferrell Jr. and Phillip Wolman, for their incredible support of my family, which made my life more stable and secure in my new home country. To Stefan Hunter, for his spiritual and material input to Pose Tech Corporation, which helped to promote the Pose Method around the world.

To Pasquale Manocchia, one of the first professionals in America to accept and support the Pose Method, whose friendship had always combined for me business and pleasure.

To professor Tim Noakes and his colleagues from Cape Town University, for their open-mindedness and greatest support of the Pose Method.

To my dear friends and associates Graham Fletcher and Connie Sol, for working with me in science, education, and coaching runners and triathletes of all levels around the world. To my colleagues and friends from USA Triathlon Coaching Committee: Cyle Sage, George Dallam, and Joe Friel, for their acceptance and promotion of the Pose Method for the sport of triathlon.

To the British Triathlon Association and its Performance Director, Graeme Maw, as well as elite athletes, Tim Don and Andrew Johns, for their great work in bringing the Pose Method to practical success.

Dr. Nicholas Romanov
Miami, Florida, October 2002

PREFACE

This is a book quite unlike any other you have ever read about running. Why? To begin with, it starts with the assumption that there are only four reasons you might pick up another book about running:

1) You want to run faster.
2) You want to avoid injury.
3) You want to lose weight.
4) Someone who had no clue what to give the runner in his or her life gave it to you.

Now, here's why this book is totally different from any other running book out there: it assumes that you don't know how to run, indeed that very few runners know how to run.

Most running books proceed from the assumption that running is not a *skill* sport but instead is a *training* sport. These books center their advice on training information -- how much to run, how hard to run, how to cross-train, what to eat, etc. All of which is valuable information, but doesn't address the central issue of *how one runs.*

Let's say that you wanted to take up a new sport such as skiing, tennis, golf, ballet or martial arts. Before you got into *training* for those sports, you would be expected to learn how to do them. It would be the most obvious thing in the world to sign up for lessons or perhaps enroll in a one-week introductory course to get started.

By contrast, the advice given most beginning runners can be summarized as follows: 1) buy a good pair of shoes & 2) don't run too hard at first. And even if a novice runner did feel the need to seek out professional guidance on running technique, as opposed to training routines, where would he or she turn? Local running clubs? Personal trainers? High school or college coaches? In the absence of any generally accepted theory of how to run, the odds against finding informed, reliable advice are astronomical.

Hence this book, The Pose Method of Running, the result of over 25 years of studying human movement and developing a singular approach to running technique. Never before has a running book started with the notion that you must first learn how to run before you begin to train for running.

Instead of loading you down with information on exercise heart rates, pacing, tactics, rest, and nutrition – all of which are very important components of the total running experience – The Pose Method of Running gets right to the heart of the matter with drills and routines designed to make you an efficient, capable runner. And once you know how to run, you'll find that all the rest of it comes very easily and naturally.

Think about it. If you can't hit a tennis ball over the net, there is no sense in playing a match. If you can't drive a golf ball past the end of the tee, why tee it up for 18? And if you can't run in a relaxed, efficient, injury-free manner, why toe the line at a local 10K or triathlon?

The Pose Method of Running in all likelihood will be easier to use for novice runners, who have no preconceived notions of technique and training, but it may have more long-term value for veteran runners who may have become frustrated by chronic injuries or failure to improve beyond a certain plateau. The novice will appreciate the simple steps necessary to adapt to the Pose Method and will literally be able to get off on the right foot in taking up the sport.

By contrast, an experienced runner brings along the baggage and expectations of many years in the sport. Someone who is used to logging 30, 40 or 50 miles a week and knows all his or her PRs (personal records) by heart may balk at the patience required to rework a running stride put in place by years and miles. If you are in this category, relax and open yourself up to the possibility that you stand a chance of becoming a much better runner once you really know how to run.

In fact, I believe that a true understanding of proper running technique will have a greater impact on your running performance than any other single factor, including the use of performance enhancing drugs. It's sad fact of our times that success in running, cycling, swimming and other endurance and strength sports is almost always put under the microscope of suspicion, so widespread has the use of illicit substances become. Even worse, this "doping" has not been limited to elite athletes but has filtered its way into high schools and jr. highs and is quite likely to be found among masters athletes who definitely should know better.

Depending on the substances involved, doping can not only lead to long term health issues, but also may actually encourage overtraining and bring on debilitating injuries in the short term. I firmly believe that you will be better served, both in the short term and the long term, by avoiding the lure of performance enhancing drugs and concentrating your efforts on a much more natural method of performance enhancement, learning how to run properly. Your performances will improve, your health won't suffer and you'll have the satisfaction of knowing that your improvement is 100% you, and not something that comes out of a pill or syringe.

Will the Pose Method of Running truly make you a faster runner who suffers fewer injuries? The answer is clearly "yes", if you master the technique and make a sensible training regime a part of your life.

Will it help you lose weight? Let's be perfectly clear – this is not a diet book and should never be construed as such. But, if you combine your sensible training regime with an equally sensible lifestyle incorporating a healthy, well-balanced diet, the proper amount of sleep and minimal indulgences in alcohol and sweets, you'll achieve the *right* weight for your body – and never even have to think about it.

And you know what? You may even thank the person who gave you this book in the first place, particularly if you grow to love running even half as much as I do.

FOREWORD

"Motions live and develop", said an outstanding Russian thinker of the 20th century, Nikolai Bernstein – the father of "Physiology of Activity" and one of the founders of Cybernetics, as the science of formation of movements and governing complex systems is known. Since Bernstein's time, the unveiling of secret life of movements and formulating the rules of non-controversial government of processes of their development became the subject of research for many scientists in the world, and the dream of many coaches.

But nature, as is well known, rarely gives away its secrets for free, and is cautious in choosing the ones worthy of such privilege. Because the one who possesses information possesses the world, or at least, can achieve much more than the one for whom knowledge is unavailable, or sadly unaccepted.

As to the secrets of such a phenomenon of movement activity as running, such chosen one appears to be Nicholas Romanov. He seems to be the first to realize that the seeming simplicity of running movements is a pretty insidious trick, and any attempts to construct a running technique in accordance with some vague postulates of sports biomechanics and the proverbial coach's "do it like me" are very often unsuccessful.

Running is a cyclical movement and any learnt error in technique is multiplied in every one of its cycles. Thus, in every running stride a poor health seeker hurts either his Achilles tendon, or the shin, or the knee joint, or the vertebrae column, or the muscles, or the ligaments. As a result, instead of stimulating the strengthening of these parts of his movement apparatus, he is bringing an almost irreparable damage to it himself.

Nicholas Romanov's method is built on strictly scientific knowledge of secrets of running in harmony with nature, and common laws of biomechanics of human movement. Its methodological integrity and non-controversial foundation is conditioned by a rational use of gravity as a natural factor of the force field of a running movement, and also by psychological-pedagogical algorhythms of formation of a clear understanding of the essence of running in learners, and the main thing, the formation of sensation of easiness and unconstrainedness of running, with acceptable energy costs.

The universality of technology of teaching and perfecting this running technique, offered by Dr. Romanov, lies in the fact that it is useful both for a sports professional, and an amateur athlete, with almost the same level of claims for sports results, and also for any lady or gentleman, just "running for health". All the groups will gain everything they need from this technology – both results and health.

The only "drawback" of this method for athletes is its incompatibility with any doping or any other prohibited stimulants for sports or physical capacity for work (efficiency). Amateur runners may have some difficulty in parting with their old belief that they can run in any way, even landing their heels on support, in order to get some load for the heart, vessels, and muscles. They will be offered a very different running style, with a different technique, and quite different sensations and health improving advantages.

Just a little note, that the lost opportunities of recreational potential of this new teaching and training technology for such countries as the USA and Russia may be measured in billions of dollars nationally, and in hundreds of thousands in family budgets of its citizens.

Closing this introduction to Nicholas Romanov's book, I caught myself on being a little envious for its future readers, who still have ahead of them happy hours of discovering its contents, and enjoying it, which for me have already passed...

Professor Vadim Balsevich,
Corresponding member of the Russian Academy of Education

INTRODUCTION

Despite the volume of scientific articles and books written about running technique, the problem of how to run, and how to teach running technique, has still not been satisfactorily addressed. This tremendous output of information and opinion remains a disjointed, even eclectic, amalgam of anecdotal observation and experience, devoid of any integral unifying concept.

As a result, the teaching process of running is something of a foster child, a process wholly dependent on the individual coach's insights, preferences and competence. Without an underlying, developed and accepted school of thought as to what constitutes proper running technique, what is taught by any given coach or instructor is pretty much the subject of personal whim.

This book is my attempt to fill this gap and present an integrated and uniform approach to running technique that can be systematically taught by instructors and coaches around the world. The concepts that form the basis of the Pose Method of Running derive not only from scientific principles, but also from observation, intuition and more than 20 years of working with runners at all ability levels.

I proceeded from the simple assumption that running, like any other human movement, must have a "best way" to be done. To find that "best way", I observed both humans and animals in their running and tried to identify the scientific principles at work in the matter of forward locomotion.

Having identified those principles, I then attempted to develop a system of human movement that would derive the maximum benefit from forces that exist in nature. It was my belief that this movement, while accomplishing essentially mechanical tasks, would be as artistic and refined as the movements that characterize ice-skating, ballet or gymnastics.

To my mind, this search for a "best way" to run was an urgent calling. If, in fact, I could design a curriculum that would allow individuals to run injury free, with better performance and, most importantly, more pleasure in their pursuit, I would have done a service to countless athletes.

Thus, I present this book as a system that will benefit both runners and their coaches. It is based on the combination of scientific reasoning and simple common sense. As such, the proof of the system will not come from strict scientific data, but the success of its repeated application over and over again.

As with other sports that one attempts to learn from a book, an individual's success in acquiring the benefits of the Pose Method of Running will rest not only on his understanding of the principles and his dedication to learning the system, but also in his or her willingness and ability to seek outside support in the endeavor.

While it is possible to learn the Pose Method by studying this book on your own, it is always better to have outside assistance. Whether it is simply a training partner or a qualified coach, having a second set of eyes to observe your technique and help you along the way will prove an invaluable asset and greatly reduce the time it takes you to adopt this new style of running.

As with any other approach to perfecting sporting endeavors, the Pose Method of Running remains very much a work in progress. As a scientist, a coach, and an author, I am always anxious to hear from anyone concerning their experiences with the Pose Method.

By sharing our knowledge and further refining this technique, I believe we can build an ever-larger community of happy, healthy and satisfied runners around the world. Your thoughts and insights could well become invaluable components of the next edition of this book, to be shared with runners of all ages and nationalities.

Dr. Nicholas Romanov

Section I

BEGINNINGS

Svetlana and Nicholas Romanov in 1972

Chapter 1

Necessity is the mother of invention.
Jonathan Swift

THE QUEST FOR PERFECT RUNNING TECHNIQUE

On a cool rainy October morning in 1977 I was returning home from the stadium of my Pedagogical University, where I had just completed a lesson in track and field with my students from the faculty of physical education. At the time, the Pedagogical University, located some 600 miles from Moscow in the city of Cheboksary, was a key cog in the Soviet Union's awesome athletic empire. Many athletes who would go on to score Olympic medals, set world records and lead powerhouse Soviet teams were enrolled at the University and did their daily training on our track and in our workout rooms.

A former student of the University myself, I was now a teacher and track & field coach. Yet, despite the many successes of our athletes and the level of prestige enjoyed by the faculty, my mood was in tune with this gloomy day, downcast and somewhat sullen.

After two years of working with my students and doing my own postgraduate studies, I realized I was caught in a paradox. On the one hand, I was now equipped with more facts and knowledge than ever before as I made the transition from competitive athlete to coach and scientist. At the same time, however, I realized that all my university education had not equipped me to teach my students such a seemingly simple exercise as running. The problem wasn't that I was a bad student or anything like that. On the contrary, I had graduated from my post-graduate studies at the top of the class and was preparing to write my doctorate in the sphere of sports science.

It was a curious dilemma. Taking full advantage of the wonderful professors and the excellent textbooks, I had been exposed to pretty much everything about running that had been accumulated in scientific and educational practice of that time. But the one thing I wanted most - a method of teaching running technique - was simply non-existent in current theory and practice.

What did exist was a body of different and generally contradictory viewpoints on the significance of running technique and the methods of teaching it. One prevailing theory held that running was second nature to humans and should not or could not be taught, since each individual's running style was preordained, essentially at birth, by his or her physical stature. Another bit of popular wisdom taught that the appropriate running technique differed for sprints, middle distances and marathons and thus required different ways of teaching it in every case.

Regardless of what side of this fence they were on, most qualified coaches and teachers appeared to agree on a certain mindset concerning running. Almost without exception, they believed that running is a simple exercise, and the best runners were those who combined the hardest training with superior genetic make-up. Following this reasoning, they felt there was little necessity to pay much attention to the specifics of running technique, unlike other track and field events like jumping, hurdling or throwing or, for that matter, other movement disciplines like ballet, karate or dancing where technique was considered of paramount importance.

4

Mastering any of these other endeavors, it was universally agreed, requires extensive involvement of intellectual and psychological efforts structuring fundamental movement, creating mental imagery and perfecting repetitive motions. At the same time, we were expected to believe that running, perhaps the most essentially human movement of all, required no technical training.

So I was puzzled by the realization that basically I didn't know what running *is,* from a biomechanical and psychological standpoint. Consequently, I didn't know either what to teach or how to teach my students. I felt simultaneously powerless and challenged. With nowhere left to turn for answers, I knew I would have to work this out for myself. The question had been ripening in me for a long time, but had never felt so urgent as it did this gray, dreary day.

I had been trying to solve the riddle of what to teach and how to teach for some time. In my quest, I had studied martial arts, dance and ballet. The latter was particularly easy, as I lived in Russia where the art and tradition of ballet were drawn to perfection. I had developed friends among the ballet dancers, and was able to watch both their training sessions and actual concert performances, thus mixing business with pleasure.

My observations of some of the world's greatest ballerinas left me with a burning question: why, is it that the movements in ballet, dances, and karate are so perfect (Fig. 1.1)? Could it be narrowed only to the number of repetitions of simple exercises? And the answer came on this dull autumn morning as a sudden flash of insight...*everything* is simple!

Simplicity itself is the key. Education in ballet, dance, martial arts, etc., is done through poses, or to be more precise, through a countless series of poses. Perfection of movement is achieved through the flow of perfectly rehearsed poses. Everything fell into place for me immediately like pieces of a puzzle. Neuromotor patterns are more easily acquired and ingrained through the space-time fixations of movements of the body, that is, through poses.

Now I was faced with another question. What were these poses in running and how could I isolate the key poses from the infinite

Fig. 1.1 Teaching technique through poses

number of poses through which the body moves in time and space? What are the criteria for choosing them? I decided to concentrate on poses emphasizing balance, compactness of the body, the readiness of muscles to do the work required to change each pose.

After years of study and observation, I at last felt I was ready to begin my life's work, to get to the very nature of running, breaking it down into its component poses and develop a system for teaching it to one and all.

Now I find myself nearly 25 years down the road from that gray October day. Following up on the decision I made, I have devoted my career to understanding one of the most fundamental human activities and developing a technique that will allow anyone to run further, faster and with significantly less stress on the body.

In those 25 years, much has happened in my life. With my wife, Svetlana, and my children, I was able to emigrate from Russia and settle in Miami, Florida. In Florida, I opened up shop as a professional running coach, working with individuals and small groups as I refined my theories of correct running technique.

At the same time, I began to develop relationships with a variety of national governing bodies and running clubs. I have worked on the national coaching committee of USA Triathlon, conducting seminars and clinics with top American triathletes and coaches. I traveled to the 2000 Olympics in Sydney, Australia as a consultant and coach to Great Britain's triathletes. In 1997, I released my first video, which continues to be sold to runners and coaches around the world.

Throughout this entire time, I have made it a point to work with runners of all ability levels, from Olympians to octogenarians. To my mind, if there really were a singular correct running technique, it would have to work for everyone, not just the elite world-class runner. In fact, while I have taken great pride in seeing the run splits of my Olympic triathletes drop significantly, I get even more satisfaction from middle age athletes who were ready to quit running due to chronic injuries and now run pain free, with faster times and less effort than they did 20 years ago.

As I have come to have a greater understanding of running, my frustration from 1977 has been transformed. Where I once struggled to come to grips with the underlying nature of running, I am now frustrated when I watch the struggles of people who want to run well, but are handicapped by a lack of knowledge about proper technique.

It is for those people that I have written "The Pose Method of Running." This book represents 25 years of thought, research, and fieldwork in the human laboratory. It is my greatest hope that it will give anyone who wants to run the freedom better than they ever thought possible. And that, in turn, their health will be better and their lives will be greatly enriched by their embrace of this most human, most elemental sport.

Chapter 2

*If you want to be healthy - run,
if you want to be handsome - run,
if you want to be smart - run.*
Ancient Greek aphorism

MY PHILOSOPHY OF RUNNING

If you thought that headline-sized promises of health, beauty and overall well being were an invention of the popular press the late 1900s, the above bit of Greek wisdom should dispel that notion. People have always sought "magic pills" to make their lives better and the Greeks were no exception. Still they had the essence right, for there is probably no other physical exercise as simple, accessible and so beneficial for human beings as running. Running *is* good for you, and when incorporated into an overall balanced lifestyle it really can go a long way toward making you healthy, handsome (or beautiful) and more thoughtful.

As an enlightened civilization, the ancient Greeks were the first to recognize the importance of running which they reflected both in their love of sports and in their art. Illustrations of runners on Greek vases portray the inherent emotional and aesthetic value of running. On these elegant vases, the artists may have been illustrating proper technique for athletes preparing for the Olympic Games or may simply have been paying homage to great heroes of the Games (Fig. 2.1).

Fig. 2.1 (a) Ancient Greeks' vision of running in art

Regardless of their purpose, it is certain that these drawings are not merely flights of artistic fancy. Quite detailed in their depiction of running technique, the drawings clearly demonstrate the difference in various athletes' efforts while running different distances at different speeds. Interestingly, they depict a general similarity of their running styles. Whether sprinting or running long distance, *the actual running technique is the same*.

I believe these similarities were not simply the emotional or aesthetic fantasies of various Greek artists. The running movements of the athletes on these vases have convinced me that the ancient Greeks intuitively or observationally had found effective elements of running technique that are as relevant today as they were thousands of years ago.

Look at these drawings and you'll see quite clearly that all the athletes run on the front part of the foot without landing on the heel. As barefoot runners, this was the obvious technique for efficiency and to prevent injury. To my mind, this barefoot running style of landing on the forefoot is the purest example of the proper nature of running...and the Greeks knew it centuries ago.

I don't believe the Greeks lacked the knowledge to comprehend the essence of running. While they may have lacked underlying scientific knowledge, they displayed a strong grasp of reality, sharp minds, and that most uncommon of virtues, common sense. As acute observers of the world, the Greeks recognized and

Fig. 2.1 (b) Another vision of running

appreciated the harmony of human interaction with nature. With their holistic approach, they valued mankind's integral role in the world. It was a time when purity of thought and action were held in high esteem.

As the Golden Age of Greece passed, mankind appeared to leave these values far behind. For a very long time, it seemed as if the value of running for running's sake was lost. Only with the revival of the Olympic Games at the end of the 1800s did we seem to return to an understanding of the value of this elemental human activity.

While both the Olympics and the Boston Marathon emerged as the 19th century gave way to the 20th, it wasn't until the 1960s that the first hint of a broad-based running boom appeared with the successes of Australian and New Zealand runners, especially after the books published by the famed New Zealand coach, Arthur Lydiard (3). In the United States, the running boom was triggered by the 1972 Olympic victory of the marathoner Frank Shorter (1).

Running no longer was considered a scholastic indulgence to be left behind at adulthood but instead came to be regarded as key component of a well-rounded healthy lifestyle. In some quarters, it was viewed almost as a panacea, a cure-all for the ills heaped upon us by modern society. As with all first loves, it seemed to have no drawbacks, only merits.

As running became a mass participation sport, it permeated all aspects of society. Where before only a lunatic fringe of adults would be caught dead running in shorts and sneakers, running shoes suddenly became de rigueur footwear for daily life. Running shoe companies blossomed overnight into marketing goliaths. Huge fields took to the streets of major cities in 5Ks, 10Ks and marathons. Running, it seemed, was on the verge of becoming a national religion.

As the first flush of the running love affair began to subside, there were the inevitable questions. If running's so good for you, people asked, why are runners always limping? If running 30 miles a week is good, won't running sixty miles a week make me even faster? The inevitable backlash came. To the sedentary, the image of a runner as a hobbled, emaciated, worn-out wreck was welcome confirmation of the couch potato life. Good thing I never started running, a "potato" could say smugly. Look what it does to you.

Rather than kill the sport, this new view of running led to sober studies of the negative and positive aspects of the sport. The newly acquired love for running didn't die. Instead, as with all great love stories, it matured into a relationship that could last a lifetime.

When the platonic stage ended, the development of running got a new healthy impulse based on the combined influences of scientific study and commercial interests. While there was now a more balanced view of the role of running in a well-rounded lifestyle, problems remained and some became quite urgent.

One of the most global challenges -- determining how to make running a truly efficient means of getting healthy, maintaining the human organism in a good condition and ready to race -- was put onto the agenda for coaches, scientists, doctors, and amateur runners themselves. The simple fact was that as running continued to grow in popularity, the incidence of running-related injuries continued to grow in lock step.

Isolating the causes of injuries and developing the means to prevent them became the topic of numerous studies, which will be discussed in subsequent chapters. While much of this discussion centered on the development of better shoes or the design of more sensible training regime, it was clear that the time had come to discuss a much more central issue. To wit, is there a universal proper running technique?

While to an outsider this might seem to be a perfectly reasonable and obvious question, within the ranks of the running community it became a hotly debated issue. The question was extensively discussed and studied from the viewpoints of common sense, coaches' experiences, and scientific research in hundreds of articles, books, and dissertations. But even as this is being written, neither scientists nor working coaches have come to a consensus on what constitutes proper running technique, much less how to teach it.

In one camp were those who believed that running is second nature, and in principle, everybody can run. Typifying that attitude is the following quote: "Through miles and miles of training I honed my leg action..." (2). In other words, the technique forms itself with significant mileage. You might call this the "presto!" school of thought. Run enough, and – presto! – you will run correctly.

Wouldn't that be a beautiful thing?

A second camp admits the existence of proper running technique, yet states paradoxically: "There is no scientifically founded ideal technique, that suits everyone... no possibilities of evaluating individual dispositions for a certain event. Absolute postulations that "this is wrong" and "this is right" are only revealing the coach's lack of insight into technical evaluation... a good coach should have insight into the theory of movement of kinesiology and ...be able to transfer observations over to an individually adapted technique". (Arno Nytro) (3). In other words, the coach has to conjure up the perfect running style unique to each individual runner.

If I were to agree with either of these points of view, I would have to admit that nature "doesn't care" how the movement of running is performed in relation to the force of gravity and the human efforts applied. But I can't agree because I believe that within nature we can find guidelines and principles that show us the proper way to perform all natural activity. I accept the philosophy of the wholeness of nature and the existence of humans as a key element within nature, which sets limits on our physiological and biomechanical functions.

Rather than accepting that there is either no correct running technique or that correct technique is unique to each individual, I felt that by studying the natural forces in which we humans exist, I could find the principles that would lead to the discovery of an ideal running technique for all humans, regardless of size, shape, age or gender.

I started with the concept that a human being, born, developed and existing within Earth's gravitational field, operates most efficiently within a certain biomechanical framework dictated by gravity. Our movements should be an integral part of this environment, organically united with it and using gravity as their source of energy, only minimally resisting its influence. Conversely, inefficiencies and injuries are caused when we break out of this framework of organic interaction with the forces of gravity and work against, rather than with, gravity.

Gravity's great power is amply demonstrated either in natural phenomena or in man's efforts to defeat it. In nature, a single misstep can trigger an avalanche and send a mass of snow sliding down a mountain at speeds of 80 mph or more. On the launch pad, we've all witnessed the tremendous power deployed by rockets seeking to escape Earth's gravitational pull. Imagine how it would affect your running to be able to transfer gravity's tremendous energy into your personal forward momentum.

To achieve the optimum running technique, the key is to make the greatest possible use of terrestrial gravity. A skilled, knowledgeable runner should be able to work with the force of gravity just as a yachtsman gains energy from the wind. A good sailor can use a headwind to move forward; a good runner taps the power of gravity to gather speed with minimum impact and expenditure of energy.

In over 25 years of studying, teaching and coaching running, I have devoted myself to taking the essentially limitless source of energy from Earth's gravity and devising a running technique that channels that gravitational energy into low impact, injury-free and, most importantly, <u>fast</u> running. I call my running technique and the method of teaching it the Pose Method of Running. Whether you are a beginner runner hoping to start out on the right foot or a veteran of 30 years on the roads and trails, this book is designed to help you run faster and more efficiently while minimizing injury and overall impact on the body.

But even more, I want you to become a complete runner, working in harmony with nature to softly and swiftly pass over the ground beneath your feet, loving every stride just as our Greek friends did so many centuries ago. When you reach this point, running becomes more than a sport, it becomes an integral part of your life. You may not instantly enjoy the Greek ideal of being healthy, handsome and smart, but you'll be well on your way.

1. Benyo, R. 1983, The Masters of the Marathon, New York, Atheneum.
2. Clayton D., 1980, Running to the top. Anderson World, Mountain View, California, p. 62.
3. Lydiard, A., G. Gilmor, 1962, Run to the Top, Wellington, A.N. and A. Reed.
4. Nitro, A., Summer 1987, "What is Correct Technique?", Track Technique, Vol. 100, P. 3195-3205.

Chapter 3

It's never too late to learn
Proverb

THE BEST TIME TO LEARN THE POSE METHOD

For most runners, regardless of experience or ability, adopting the Pose Method of Running will represent a major change in running style. And because runners tend to focus on weekly mileage and P.R.s (personal record times) it can be very tempting to ignore the technique to "get a long run in" or "run a quick 5K." Thus, you should schedule your conversion to the Pose Method when your expectations for performance are the lowest – your off-season.

Like swimming and cycling, the very simple movements that comprise your running style have been reinforced throughout literally millions of repetitions. The old saw "you never forget how to ride a bicycle" applies equally to running. Once you have developed a personal style, generally with no instruction whatsoever, the process of repetition called "overlearning" cements that style as a part of you, every bit as distinctive as your own signature.

In your efforts to change that style, you will find that any attempt to run either hard or far will cause you subconsciously to revert to what feels normal to you. This effect is increased as your fatigue grows. The farther you go, the more you will tend to run like you used to, thus compromising your efforts to imprint the Pose Method as your new style.

This is very difficult for most runners to accept. They naturally feel that they will lose fitness if they don't get in their weekly 40 miles. If that's the case with you, find something else like cycling or swimming to do to maintain your fitness as you focus your running efforts on the drills that will make the Pose Method your new running signature.

By starting your Pose Method transition when your expectations are lowest, you'll be able to adapt to the new style with minimal anxiety and be ready to fly when it's time to step up your mileage. And, as a side benefit, your replacement exercise will have strengthened your whole body and freshened your mind for the hard work of running hard.

Chapter 4

The Racers run smoothly,
with a fine tuned stride
like a Wankel rotary engine.
No wasted energy,
no fighting the street
or bouncing along like a jogger.
These people flow,
and they flow very fast.
Hunter S. Thompson

BEFORE YOU START – A SIMPLE TEST

Whether you're an experienced runner seeking greater performance or an absolute neophyte just starting out in this wonderful sport, there's a simple test to try before proceeding with The Pose Method of Running. It's absolutely free and it doesn't cost anything, except perhaps a couple of hours of sleep on a weekend morning.

Locate a running race in your community, a 5k or 10K will suffice, and plan to attend as a spectator. For this test, you won't need a stopwatch or a roster of the competitors; all you'll need are your eyes and ears. What you'll be testing is the widely held theory that there is no one correct way to run.

This theory holds that running technique is personal and unique for each individual. In fact, in some variations of this theory, it is even considered dangerous to attempt to modify a "natural" running stride and that to do so will invariably wind up resulting in injury or diminished performance.

For the start of the race, position yourself perhaps a half mile from the starting line, at a point where the early showboaters have faded from the front and the "real" runners have assumed the lead. As the front-runners approach, watch them as a group. Note the economy of movement, the benign expressions on their faces, the almost Zen-like concentration.

As the lead pack gets to your position, switch your focus from what you see to what you hear. The collected footfall of the leaders is soft, so soft in fact that sound of their breathing may be louder than that of their feet hitting the ground.

Fig. 4.1 "Stomp"

20

Keep listening as the back markers approach. Where the leaders swept past with only a whisper of rapid foot taps, you now hear much more recognizable thuds. The collective breathing is more labored – and this only a half-mile into the race – but the dominant sound is now the thumping of feet on the ground, pavement pounding at its best (Fig. 4.1).

Journalist Hunter S. Thompson, whose quote from his book <u>The Curse of Lono</u> opened this chapter, vividly described this transition from "The Racers" to "The Runners" as he described the Honolulu Marathon:

The Runners are different. Very few of them flow, and not many run fast. And the slower they are, the more noise they make. By the time the four-digit numbers came by, the sound of the race was disturbingly loud and disorganized. The smooth rolling hiss of the Racers had degenerated into a hell broth of slapping and pounding feet.

With that image in your mind, make your way to a point about a quarter mile from the finish line, a spot too far from the line for wild sprints to start but where the full effects of the race are clearly evident in the form of the runners. At the beginning of the race, you immersed in a group image of fast versus slow runners. Now, with the pack being spread out, you can pay more attention to individual styles.

The first thing you may notice is that the runners whose form has degenerated the least over the course of the race are the ones winning the race. And while their rhythm may have deteriorated somewhat, they're still moving economically, still devoid of expression and still concentrating. Despite the great efforts they have made, the winners tend to show the least effects of the race – at least while they're still running.

As the rest of the pack proceeds toward the finish line, begin to watch the running styles of the various entrants. You'll see all kinds of wild stuff – flailing arms, stumbling feet, twisting bodies. Some

21

runners are clearly landing on their heels; others are all the way up on their toes. The struggle is much more evident on almost all the faces.

What conclusions can you draw from this test? While we shouldn't expect any blinding flashes of insight, it's fair to say that the best runners run more like each other than the worst runners. You could also say that the best runners appear to be more efficient and more focused. But most importantly, given the wide disparity of running styles on display, it is clear that human beings aren't gifted by nature with an innate, correct running stride. To get that is going to take a little work.

Section II

THE CASE FOR
THE POSE METHOD

Chapter 5

The third law of running injuries:
Each running injury indicates
that the athlete has reached his
breakdown point.
Tim Noakes

ELIMINATE INJURIES FROM YOUR RUNNING

Why should I bother learning a new way to run?

That's a fair question and if you're not convinced that there is value in learning the Pose Method, then you're certainly not going to follow through on the process of changing your running style. The value of anything is determined by its practical applicability. In other words, how does the introduction of something new improve our ability to accomplish a given task? What does it give us that we didn't already have?

Ask just about any runner what they would like to see happen in their running and the answer you'll get would likely be some variation of, "I'd like to run faster, farther, with less effort and fewer injuries."

The answer you won't get is, "I'd like to become a more efficient running machine," but that's really the ultimate goal, to turn yourself into a swifter human being, impervious to the nagging injuries that drag all of us down. No, I'm not going to say that the Pose Method will instantly turn Joe or Jane Average Weekend Warrior into a world record-setting Olympian, but it will give you that knowledge and the mechanics to significantly enhance your performance and reduce your injuries.

There are three primary limiting factors in our running performance: injuries, technique, and personal limitations. Before actually introducing you to the technique of the Pose Method, I want to talk about how it was designed to address each of these limitations. In this chapter, I'll start with the big bugaboo – injuries.

Given that consistency is the most important component of any training regime and that injuries are the biggest enemy of consistency, let's talk a little about just how big of a problem injuries are and see how the Pose Method addresses that problem.

Anyone with running experience knows that injuries are as much a part of the sport as running shoes, socks and shorts. It is just generally accepted that injuries like stress fractures, sore knees, tweaked ankles, strained Achilles' tendons, lower back pain and plantar fasciitis are part of the total running experience. Interestingly, this situation with running injuries doesn't seem to have changed since the beginning of the running boom in 1970 up until the present time, despite vast resources devoted to improved running shoe design and the evolution of theoretically smarter training regimes.

The same sad statistics crop up in article after article. Back in 1977, an article in "Runner's World" magazine noted that two out of every three runners suffer injuries every year which lead to interruption or reduction of training and racing activity (2). Twenty years later, Gary Guten wrote in his book Running Injuries that more recent studies found "the relative incidence of running injuries similar to that of earlier studies" (1). Given that there are an estimated 33.7 million regular runners in the U.S. alone, this is

26

an astonishing situation (5). Run the numbers and you see that something like 22 million American runners have their training slowed or interrupted by injuries every year. Ouch!

While the number and frequency of running injuries remained consistent over the years, they seem to have migrated up the leg. In the '70s, the greatest proportion of injuries seemed to be concentrated in the feet and lower leg (3). As we moved into the '90s, those injuries were reduced, but that reduction was offset by an increase in problems with shin splints and knee injuries (4)

If we accept that improvements in shoe design and technology explain why foot and lower leg injuries were reduced, what are we to make of the corresponding increase in shin and knee problems?

In Gary Guten's book, he notes the four factors that contribute to sports injuries: change, alignment, twisting, and speed. The first one, "change", is very common with runners and refers to a sudden increase of mileage, distance, frequency, or intensity of training by more than 10% per week. In other words, the runner wants to see some fast improvement and instead commits the most basic training error of all, overdoing it and winding up injured instead of faster.

Factor number two, "alignment", literally means "arrangement in a straight line" and describes what kind of anatomical structure the athlete has. Well aligned athletes, born with straight legs, straight spines, and straight arms, tend to have fewer injuries. The third factor, "twisting" is less relevant for runners, but a major factor for golfers, gymnasts and volleyball players. The fourth one refers to fast running, often a major culprit when a runner makes a too quick transition from a distance base phase to interval training.

Additional specific factors in running injuries include the surface and the shoes. Taken together, all these factors can work separately or together to cause or intensify injuries. So there's a lot out there that can do us in and create problems when we're running, but I think that all these factors are still missing the point.

In all these studies, there is virtually no attempt to correlate running injuries to running technique. In a racquet sport such as tennis, a teaching pro might spot a flaw in a student's serve and quite quickly say that the flaw will lead to a shoulder problem. In running, where there is no consensus about proper technique, it is very difficult to establish correlation between a certain running style and a likely injury that will result.

Further, given that the vast majority of amateur runners are self-coached, there are few opportunities for even obvious flaws to be caught and corrected. And even when a runner is working with a coach, the teaching tends to be eclectic and depends heavily on the personality of the coach, his knowledge, experience, and personal preferences.

It all adds up to a very strange situation. There have been continuous studies of running, running shoes have been vastly improved, the average runner knows more about training and racing than ever before, yet the frequency of running injuries remains unchanged! Doesn't it indicate the absence of something important in the preparation of runners?

And just on the level of common sense, it should be clear that a correct, perfect model of technique would influence directly not only the level of running performance, but would also serve as an effective means of injury prevention. Let's proceed from the assumption that while an injury may be specific to a certain body part, it really constitutes a failure on the part of the whole body. When the body is functioning properly, with all systems operating in the correct alignment and in unison, there should be no injuries. However, when something in that movement is incorrect, the body breaks out of the framework of its normal operation and something "breaks."

It could be a simple situation like a stubbed toe. Having accidentally kicked a table leg with a bare foot in the morning, the runner assumes that his $100 pair of training shoes will provide ample protection and heads out for the normal evening five-miler.

28

A week later, the pain in the toe has subsided, but guess what, a new, much more insidious pain has entrenched itself in the knee. A minor problem combined with our runner's insistence on sticking to a normal training routine has now led to a potentially serious injury.

What happened, of course, is that our dedicated runner subconsciously made very slight alterations to his normal running stride to minimize the impact on the sore toe. Over the course of a week's training, just this slight alteration put undue pressures on the opposite knee, resulting in connective tissue damage.

When you look at it from an engineering standpoint, the human body really is a marvel, able to sustain a variety of smooth movements both over land and in the water. To do so, all the various parts and systems in the body have to work both individually and together to support that movement.

As we have seen with the above example, when just one of those parts or systems gets slightly out of whack, the entire body is thrown out of balance and there is a risk of injury. The running "machine" has gone out of tune and is at risk of breaking down completely.

The technique of any movement, including running, is the sum total of all of the elements of the training process. Whatever we develop, be it muscle groups, the heart, the respiratory system, the psyche...all this potential and effort is aimed at performing a simple, repeatable movement. Whether this training is focused on a specific singular motion such as a high jump or a repetitive motion like running, it all boils down to perfecting the art of movement.

So, all roads lead to Rome. If we are going to run injury free and effectively, then we must develop a technique that is most efficient for the human body. And if we allow that technique to deteriorate, this will both lead to greater energy expenditures necessary to sustain the intended pace and increase the likelihood that the runner will suffer injury.

Building upon my insights from that bleak rainy day in 1977, I began to develop a model for the perfect running technique. As I mentioned at the end of the last chapter, the necessary elements would include balance, compactness of the body and the readiness of the muscles to do the work required to change each pose. To this, I now added the requirement that the poses involved in this new running technique would minimize the risk of injury.

Now, looking at the act of running as a technical exercise having its own biomechanical structure, and being in the same category of movement as jumping, throwing or dancing, it was easy to refute the widely held notion that running is second nature to humans. From this perspective, it becomes obvious that most people haven't had the correct running habits from birth. Far from being an innate habit, running is clearly an acquired skill. And just like any other skill, it can be either poorly performed or perfected.

As a coach and a scientist, I realized the need for a method combining science and practice that could be explained and taught quickly and easily to runners of any level. After much analysis of human biomechanics, I concluded that the principal pose in the ideal running technique is the vertical S-like stance on one leg. The running itself is performed utilizing the change of support from one leg to another, in the pose of running. Thus, my Pose Method of Running, as I came to call it in the mid-'70s, incorporates two simple elements: the running pose, and the change of support in the pose of running.

When designing the Pose Method, my idea was to take what nature gives us and use it to great effect. I wanted the runner to get the maximum benefit out of the gratuitous forces of gravity, muscle elasticity and inertia and minimize voluntary muscular efforts that require the expenditure of energy. In other words, the best running style should be the easiest way to run. And if we run easily, taking advantage of the energy found in nature and minimizing human energy, then we will increase speed and endurance and at the same time reduce injuries.

1. Guten, N.G., editor, 1997, Running Injuries, Philadelphia, W.B. Saunders Company, pp. 61-65.
2. Krissoff, W.B., and Ferris, W.D., 1979, Runner's Injuries, Physician Sports Med., 7:55-64.
3. MacIntyre, S.G., at al, 1991, "Running Injuries: a clinical study of 4173 cases. Clinical Journal of Sports Medicine, New York, 1(2), pp. 81-87.
4. Stanly L. James, Donald C. Jones, 1990, Biomechanical Aspects of Distance Running Injuries, Biomechanics of Distance Running, editor P.R. Cavanagh, Champaign, IL, Human Kinetics, pp. 249-269.
5. www.AmericanSportsData.com/ss_participation4.htm.

Chapter 6

*The world hates change,
yet it is the only thing
that has brought progress.*
Charles F. Kettering

IMPROVE YOUR PERFORMANCE

Will the Pose Method of Running really make me a faster runner?

I suppose that's really the million dollar question and the answer is, "By itself, No!"

Surprised? Don't be. The only thing that can make you a faster runner is – you. But by learning and adapting to the Pose Method, you will have a powerful tool in your arsenal that will allow you to become a faster runner at any distance.

To do so, veteran runners will have to overcome an understandable reluctance to meddle with a running style that to them feels quite natural. Even if you are subject to frequent injuries, any time you're not injured and you're running well, you will undoubtedly think to yourself, "If it ain't broke, don't fix it."

It's a common sentiment, but one that will consign you to a level of performance not much different than where you are today. If you want to raise your game to a different level, as they say, major changes will have to be made. Perhaps the story of two world-class athletes in vastly different sports will help you make the decision.

In 1997, Tiger Woods had swept through the world of professional golf as a hurricane assaults the Carolinas. Young and full of fire, he had wrapped up an astonishing amateur career with three consecutive U.S. Amateur titles. Moving into the ranks of the PGA, he won two of his first seven starts and then smashed the tournament record as he ran away from the field at the world's most prestigious tournament, the Masters.

While the golf media and his fellow competitors virtually ceded tour dominance to Tiger for the next 20 years, he reached a different conclusion. With insight so rare for one so young, he looked at his own golf game and determined that he lacked the solid foundation he would need to maintain his performance over the years. Far from being prepared to dominate, Tiger felt his success was due to his speed and reflexes, qualities that naturally diminish over time.

So rather than ride out his hot streak, Tiger Woods cut down on his competitive schedule and went back to his teaching pro to totally rebuild his game. It was a tremendous gamble for someone towering over his sport and during the interregnum that followed there were whispers about his staying power as other golfers began winning tournaments.

But gradually over the next 18 months, the pieces of Tiger's new game began to fall together, just as he said they would. In mid-1999, with David Duval ensconced as golf's #1 ranked player, Tiger went on a new streak, winning five consecutive tournaments and threatening the all-time mark of the legendary Byron Nelson, set in a far less competitive era. It took tremendous self-knowledge and pure guts to do what he did, but Tiger Woods showed that the courage to change can have tremendous rewards.

34

His subsequent performances, including the so-called "Tiger Slam," where he won four consecutive major championships (The U.S. Open, The British Open, The PGA and The Masters) have only validated the changes he made back in 1997 and 1998.

A far different challenge faced cyclist Lance Armstrong as he approached the 1999 professional season in Europe. A child prodigy triathlete, Armstrong demonstrated tremendous talent on the bicycle and made the switch to cycling full-time in his late teens. Racing on the European circuit, he became the first American to win a World Cup classic and then beat a top field including Tour de France champion Miguel Indurain to win cycling's World Championship at age 22. With stage victories in the Tour de France and a much-publicized million-dollar Triple Crown victory in the United States, Lance Armstrong had clearly assumed the role held by three-time Tour winner Greg Lemond as the greatest American cyclist.

Armstrong's greatest asset as a cyclist was his incredible ability to accelerate over short steep climbs, "walls" in the cycling vernacular. In was attack on the famed Manayunk Wall in Philadelphia that brought him the third of his Triple Crown wins as he claimed the U.S. Professional Cycling Championship. And when he won the 1993 World Championship in Oslo, it was a similar attack that allowed him to distance a chase group of 10 riders led by Indurain, who would go on to finish second.

However, the power that brought success to Armstrong in one-day events was seen as liability in the grand tours of cycling – the Tours of Italy, Spain and, most importantly, France. To win one of the grand tours, explosive power was tertiary to the ability to ride day after day in the high mountains and the ability to push it to the limit in the crucial time trial stages. The book on Lance Armstrong was that he was a great one-day rider, but he would never be a champion in a three-week tour.

All of that seemed secondary in 1996 when, after a disappointing performance in the Olympic Games road race in Atlanta, Armstrong was diagnosed with testicular cancer. As later tests revealed the cancer had spread to his abdomen, lungs and brain, survival, not winning bike races, became his primary challenge.

With aggressive treatment and a remarkably positive attitude, Armstrong beat the cancer and in 1998 made his return to the pro circuit in Europe. At first his performances were uneven and he even left cycling for a while, uncertain he would ever return. But by the end of the 1998 season, it was clear Lance Armstrong was back, when, in a five-week period, he raced to consecutive 4th places in the three-week Tour of Spain, the World Championship Time Trial and the World Championship road race.

Chapter 7

*The only true law is that
which leads to freedom.*
Richard Bach

THE FREEDOM TO RUN YOUR BEST

Freedom? Seems like an odd concept to mix in with injuries and technique when we're talking about running, doesn't it? Yes, we are all free to run within the constraints of our daily lives, but how many of us actually permit ourselves the psychological freedom to run the way we would like to run? The answer, painfully, is very few.

The psychological freedom to perform at a higher level rests within all of us, but as human beings we habitually place limits on that freedom (Fig. 7.1). You may say to yourself, "I could never run a 10K under 40 minutes," or "I don't need to do interval training." In order to place a comfort level on your expectations, you have voluntary placed limits on your ultimate performance. You have chosen not to be free.

Within the limits you have set on yourself, you now have the ability for self-satisfaction. Having determined that you can't run the 10K

Fig. 7.1. "Restrictions of Life

under 40 minutes, you can be enormously satisfied if you run a 40:30, thinking you've run just about as well as you can run. And by avoiding interval work, you can be happy that you always feel good and never "hurt" when you run. Still, without your self-imposed limitations you know, on a subconscious level, that you could do better.

Of course, it is impossible to be absolutely free when it comes to running. Life does impose limitations – social considerations like family, work, and community act along with physical concerns such as weather, the topography, and gravity to define the parameters of your possible peak performance.

Given the reality of life, your psychological freedom is your ability to minimize the effect of the natural limitations and rise to your highest level. To do so, you must consciously work on developing your mind-set and psyche for running.

First, you have to consider the source of these natural limitations. You may feel guilty taking the time out to run when you could be spending time with your children or doing chores around the house. You may been raised in a family that didn't value exercise and felt that running was a waste of your time compared to learning to play an instrument or work on your studies. You may even feel that you are not quite ready to take on a task as challenging as running or entering a competitive race. Your personal limitations may be very current or they may have been inculcated over the years.

Similarly, in the physical realm, you may feel that you are too heavy to run or that your knees won't take the pounding. It may be too hot for you in the summer, too cold in the winter or you may think that there is no good place to run where you live.

And if you already run, but avoid intervals, that may be a self-imposed limitation, but it may also be valid. If your running technique is flawed, intervals will not only "hurt" in the sense that they can bring you momentary suffering, but they can lead to injury.

In all these cases, the key to overcoming your limitations is knowledge. Knowledge of your circumstances gives you the wisdom to successfully integrate your running into your family and home life. Knowledge of proper running gear, hydration and rest permits you to run in any conditions. Knowledge of your neighborhood and your hometown allows you to find suitable training routes.

Most importantly, knowing *how* to run gives you the possibility to run freely. When you know your body and you know how to run, you will have no fear of overtraining, no fear of injuries. You can be truly free to run long distances, to run hard intervals. You can be free to run faster than you ever have before.

To reach your peak performance, you must have the psychological freedom to overcome your limitations. This starts with the foundation of a proper running technique. Belief in your technique then gives you the confidence to move past your limitations and explore your true potential.

As you move forward with your development of strength, speed, flexibility, coordination, and endurance, your mind-set will become much stronger. With a strong mind, you will no longer fear running too much mileage, running too hard during workouts or doing the training exercises that will give your body the ability to perform at a higher level. Rather than fear or shy away from the pain of an extremely hard effort, your new mind-set will enjoy the experience as you see just how hard you can go.

Where once subconsciously you might have feared going out to achieve a new 10K PR, your new knowledge and freedom will allow you to look forward to and relish the experience as you set new personal standards. Yes, it will still hurt, but the momentary pain of an honest effort will be masked by the enormous satisfaction of your personal achievement.

How is all this going to happen for you? How are you going to overcome a lifetime of limitations to suddenly become a wiser, stronger, more confident and ultimately faster runner? Well, it's not going to be sudden. It's going to be an evolutionary process that involves patience, learning, focus and determination. At the outset you may feel like you're backing up as you go from a regimen of 30 or 40 miles a week to one that is short on distance and long on drills. But as you work through the steps involved in learning the Pose Method of Running you will find a total package coming together for you.

Nagging injuries will fade away and be forgotten. What were once maximum speeds will soon become sustainable paces. Your fear of running intervals will be replaced by an excited anticipation as your next interval workout approaches. Impending races will no longer be a source of dread, but opportunities to rewrite your personal record book. You will have the freedom to succeed.

Chapter 8

THE INCREDIBLE LIGHTNESS OF RUNNING

Chances are you know a lot of people who stopped running or considerably scaled back their weekly mileage because their bodies simply couldn't take the pounding. Or perhaps you have done the same, having grown tired of constant soreness and pain, the shin splints, the aching knees, the bruised heels or even the dreaded plantar fasciitis.

Without a doubt, if you suffer these maladies then cutting back on your running brings welcome relief. But wouldn't you really rather continue to run, if only you could avoid all the discomfort? Of course you would. The key is to stop pounding the pavement and start passing lightly over it.

When you run in the most common manner of landing on your heel, rolling across the foot and then toeing off, you're leaving the full weight of your body on your feet and the ground for the maximum amount of time possible.

To begin, in order to land on your heel, your foot has to be way out in front of your body (Fig. 8.1). As you roll across your foot, your full body weight comes crashing down on your foot through a leg that is now straight and fully extended, with no ability to absorb shock. Then, as you toe off, you are literally trying to kick your body forward through your extended toes. No wonder you hurt all over.

Fig. 8.1. "The Leg Ahead"

The result of this body battering is quite audible, as a simple test will reveal. Just find a quiet stretch of pavement away from the noise of traffic and listen to your foot strike as your run at various speeds. *Thud, thud, thud.* That's the sound of your body weight being magnified as you pound your way down the road.

By contrast, when you master the Pose Method of Running, you will experience the Incredible Lightness of Running. The knees always stay slightly bent, to fully absorb any road shock. The foot strikes the pavement only at the forefoot and stays on the ground for the minimum amount of time possible. And most importantly, the foot strike comes directly below the body and not out in front.

Instead of pounding the pavement, you now are virtually hovering above it. Listen. Instead of *thud, thud, thud* you now hear *tap, tap, tap*. Focus on the tapping. As your leg speed increases, you want the tapping to become less and less audible. Each brief tap is your only contact with the ground. You are no longer thudding the full weight of your body <u>through</u> the pavement, you're keeping it suspended <u>above</u> the pavement. This is the Incredible Lightness of Running.

Section III

THE CONCEPTS OF
THE POSE METHOD

Chapter 9

*You teach best what
you most need to learn.*
Richard Bach
Men learn while they teach.
Seneca

TEACHING YOURSELF THE POSE METHOD
OF RUNNING

As a coach used to working with athletes in a concentrated hands-on environment, it is enormously frustrating to know I can't meet and work with everyone who would like to learn the Pose Method. It also presents a great challenge to translate 25 years of experience into text, pictures and illustrations that will teach you how to teach yourself this new approach to running. However, once you accept the basic premise that running is in fact a skill sport, you'll find that many of the basic precepts of the Pose Method are just plain common sense, on which I will rely whenever possible.

For your part, as an individual dedicated to improving his or her running, the challenge will be to fulfill the role of both teacher and student. Somewhat like a substitute teacher who has been thrown into a classroom in a subject outside his expertise, the teacher in you needs to stay a chapter or two ahead of your other role as a student. As the two quotes by Bach and Seneca at the head of this chapter indicate, by combining the role of teacher and student, you will greatly enhance your quest at adopting the Pose Method.

From a practical standpoint, this means fully comprehending the concepts of the Pose Method that will be covered later in this section. As the teacher, you can then talk yourself as the student through the physical drills of the Pose Method that follow in Sections Four and Five with complete confidence. Feel free to address yourself in the second person, i.e. "Okay, what you need to do here is…" In other words, teach your body to do what your mind has already visualized.

Perhaps the most important factor in learning the Pose Method will be your willingness to consider, accept and teach yourself elements of the Pose Method that do not conform to conventional views. After all, if the Pose Method *was* conventional, there would hardly be a need for this book.

When we get into these non-conventional areas, you'll need to make extra effort to comprehend the logic and then translate that comprehension from intellectual acceptance to physical sensations that lead to a specific performance of movements.

As discussed above, first you need to accept that running is a skill, an art of movement. As with all other movement arts including dance, ballet, tennis, swimming, or martial arts, it must be taught. Of course, there is such a thing as spontaneous mastery and acquisition of technique. Natural selection dictates that some people just can paint, sing, dance or run beautifully without any special education. That's just the way it is. But even in these cases, peak performance can only be achieved through the tutelage of a teacher or in structured self-education.

The same natural selection that gifts certain individuals with artistic or athletic prowess means that there have always been some runners who used the techniques I have embodied in the

Pose Method. Despite the fact that there was no accepted running technique and no one to teach it, some runners just run this way naturally.

When Michael Johnson electrified the world with his Gold Medal performances in the 200 and 400 meter runs at the 1996 Olympics in Atlanta, television analysts and sports writers made numerous references to his "short, choppy strides" and his erect running stance. It was clear watching video replays that Johnson's technique was utterly different than all of his competitors who all had longer strides and more of a forward lean. The commentators mentioned the difference, but never really seemed to analyze it.

After the games, Johnson's coach, Clyde Hart, mentioned in a Runner's World article that he found Johnson's style to be unusual and possibly even strange (1). However, Hart was wise enough to see that the style obviously worked for Michael Johnson, so he never suggested that he change it.

At the other end of the spectrum, another Olympic champion and a world record holder at the 5K and 10K distances, Haile Gebrselassie, told Running Times Magazine, how his technique was formed. "When I was 14 or 15," he said, "I remember my brother tried to encourage me by giving me a pair of running shoes. But I threw them away, because I was used to running with bare feet, and the shoes were too heavy" (2).

What makes this interesting is that these two runners, arguably the greatest sprinter and distance runner, respectively, in history, share an almost identical technique. As was the case with the ancient Greeks, long barefoot runs forged Gebrselassie's style. Try running barefoot for just a few moments on the grass and you'll realize a barefoot runner is not one who lands heel first. A barefoot runner lands on the ball of the foot and does so as lightly as possible. While I don't know where Johnson got his style, he too lands on the ball of his foot. And those short, choppy strides that captivated the Olympic viewing audience really indicate the rapid turnover that drove him to a breathtaking time of 19.32 seconds in the Olympic 200, quite possibly the greatest single run in history.

If you were to approach either Johnson or Gebrselassie and say "I see you use the Pose Method of Running," I am quite sure that neither one would have the slightest idea what you were talking about. But the fact is that each of them lands on the ball of the foot, employs a compact stride, minimizes extraneous movement and keeps both legs bent at all times. Natural selection – and wise coaching – has made them poster athletes for the Pose Method.

To this point I've only explained the concepts that comprise the Pose Method. This is because I want you to develop a sense of the history, the thought and the possibilities inherent in its development. Unless you know why you are doing something, it is very difficult to dedicate yourself to it. And the process of changing a deeply ingrained physical habit like a running stride is as much mental as it is physical. No doubt there will be many times when you will just want to drop the whole thing, rush out the front door and run five miles your "natural" way.

So really, there are two things I don't want to happen. First, I don't want you to experiment with the Pose Method before you have a total *intellectual* understanding of what it is. And second, I don't want you to abandon your attempt to master it before you have truly experienced the *physical* sensations of the method. In the next chapter we'll talk about the methods by which we acquire new knowledge and then, and only then, will you be ready to begin the teaching/learning process.

1. Wischnia, Bob, 1996, "Point To Point", Runner's World, October, Vol. 31, No. 10, p. 16
2. Mackay, Duncan, 1998, "Record Quest", Running Times, July/August, No. 250, pp. 58-62

Chapter 10

Whatever you cannot understand,
you cannot possess.
Goethe

THINKING...SEEING...FEELING

People learn by different means. Some think things through. Some visualize. And some play it by feel (Fig. 10.1). Actually, all of us use elements of each process, but to varying degrees, each of us allowing one method to be dominant. The challenge in preparing you for the process of self-teaching the Pose Method is to make sure that no matter how you learn, you'll have a sound and easily followed approach as you move from the intellectual precepts of the Method to its physical application.

We'll call the intellectual side "what" and the physical side "how." "What" and "how" really do exist independently, but must be unified in the process of learning the Pose Method. We'll consider them separately for the sake of simplicity of explanation, but will combine them later into an integrated process for your self-education.

The process of your running education will hinge on a set of special exercises but, just an importantly, it will progress from a complex of knowledge and ideas on movement and a set of

51

visualizations of movement all the way to a set of sensations and feelings from movement. We will create different structures of movement, specifically of running movement. Our ultimate goal is a biomechanical structure of running incorporating the structures of thought, visualization, and sensations. Then we'll unify these structural frames of time and space into a holistic package – the act of perfect running.

Fig. 10.1. Perceptions we use in teaching of movement

Our friends the ancient Greeks refer to structure as the law of uniting the parts of the whole. To successfully complete your running education, we must activate all three structures involved in this process. To be honest, it's not going to be easy.

First, we have to distill the key components of "what" and "how" into explanations that you can comprehend, no matter whether you learn by thinking, visualizing or feeling.

For the thinkers among us, we have to demonstrate the logic of combining certain areas of knowledge into an integrated whole. To a "thinker," the explanation begins something like this: *running is the transfer of the body horizontally in time and space. This transfer is accomplished through the alternation of poses from one leg to the other, again and again.* The education of the "thinker" then proceeds in owner's manual fashion, with every step in the running process carefully articulated. Along the way, we mix in scientific explanations of gravitational forces and the student's own personal body of experience and we arrive at the proper running movements.

On the other hand, the process for a "visualizer" is quite different. For a visualizer, we employ appropriate visual or aural cues and images from nature. A visualizer might be told to run like a cheetah, jump like a kangaroo or ride gravity like a sail catching the wind.

Finally, to those who learn by feeling, we speak of sensations of time, space, balance, acceleration, muscular contractions, and relaxations, etc. All these sensations have a place in the structure of running. While beginning runners have minimal development of key sensory experiences, elite runners often have highly acute awareness of their minutest movements. Do you learn by feeling? Here are some simple tests to check your own awareness of time and space.

Fig. 10.2. Checking your time sense by stopping the stop watch in 5 seconds without looking at it

Try stopping a stopwatch at 5 seconds without looking (Fig. 10.2.) Good runners often come with a tenth of a second, time after time. How did you do? You may be shocked to find yourself stopping the watch anywhere from three to seven seconds. Your sense of time may not be what you thought it was.

Here's another test for the senses. Close your eyes and ask a friend to place some of his fingertips very lightly on your arm. Then tell your friend how many points of contact you feel. Your answer may surprise both of you. Finally, try to hold your balance in the position shown in Figure 11.2. Not so easy, huh?

What these simple experiments show us is that we are all different in our innate ability to distinguish key elements of time, space and balance. In turn, that shows that we will all be different in our abilities to master a new skill that involves balanced movement through time and space.

Just as a good musician easily distinguishes fine nuances of sound, and an artist "knows" color, a good runner must learn to be acutely aware of time, space, balance and touch to be able to coordinate his running movements in the best way possible.

To properly assimilate the Pose Method, we have to rely on the concepts of thinking, visualizing, and sensations of running. We'll start with "what" and "how," but end up knowing, seeing and feeling.

Chapter 11

> *When you understand one thing*
> *through and through,*
> *you understand everything.*
> Shunyro Suzuki

THE RUNNING POSE

At the heart of the Pose Method of Running is what I call the Running Pose. This is the single instance in the entire cycle of the running stride that is critical to perfect running. Master the concepts, the image and the feel of the Running Pose and you will be positioned to develop your running to a new level. Fail to master the pose and you will progress no further.

If you analyze the movement of any body through time and space, you will clearly see that the body passes through an infinite number of positions. Most of the positions (or poses) are transitional movements and are the result, not the cause, of proper positioning. The key to isolating the Running Pose was to study footage of the world's best runners and search for the single position that would predetermine the biomechanics of the preceding and subsequent movements, in effect triggering perfect running (Fig. 11.1).

55

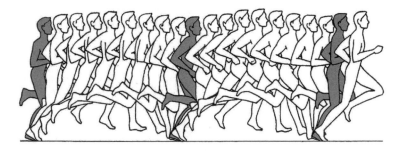

*Fig. 11.1 Running stride - as a sequence of poses
(Dark color indicates the pose)*

Not only would this position trigger proper performance, but it would permit the runner to concentrate only on the exact movements required for perfect running and remove the very thought of superfluous or unnecessary movements. If we could find the perfect Running Pose, we could get to the heart of the matter, so to speak, and focus all of our energy on doing what is absolutely necessary to move our body forward through time and space and waste no energy on inconsequential movement.

Precisely this ability of certain poses to integrate the whole chain of preceding and subsequent movements into one whole laid the foundation of the Pose Method. Analysis of film footage of the world's best runners confirmed the original hypothesis, that there is a pose that satisfies all the requirements to serve as the basis for perfect running. This analysis showed that all running technique could be formed with the help of just one position or pose, the "Running Pose" (Fig. 11.2).

The Running Pose is distinguished from the thousands of positions in the running cycle in three critical ways: balance, potential energy and resilience.

In the Running Pose, the runner is perfectly balanced on his or her support. A direct line of the body goes from the head, through the shoulders and buttocks all the way to the ball of the foot that is in

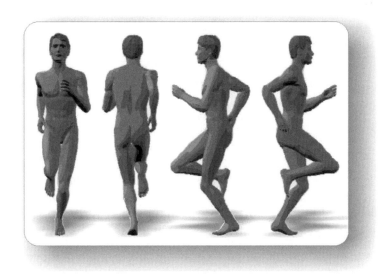

Fig. 11.2 Running Pose. Four Views

contact with the ground (Fig. 11.3). The heel of the support leg is slightly higher than the ball of the foot and may even lightly touch the ground, but the weight of the body always rests only on the front part of the foot and not on the toes (Fig. 11.4).

By running in a position of perfect balance, the runner wastes no energy in extraneous movements that only serve to correct balance. That is why so much attention will be paid at the beginning to perfecting the running pose. In the same way that figure skaters spend so much time with school figures before doing spins and jumps, you must master the simplicity of the Running Pose before moving on to the intricacy of actually running.

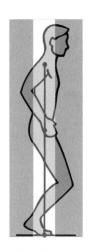

Fig. 11.3 Vertical Alignment of the body – head, shoulder, hip, foot

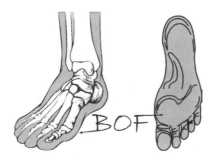

Fig. 11.4 The foot contact with the ground – body weight placement on the ball of the foot

The Running Pose is also the most compact and "ready-to-go" position of the body, allowing its most effective movements during its interaction with the support. In other words, it is in the position of maximum potential energy. Like a ball on the edge of a table, a body in the Running Pose is ready to roll, so to speak (Fig. 11.5).

Finally, the Running Pose is the pose of resilience. The body is in a spring-like with all key muscle groups relaxed and ready to fire (Fig. 11.6). The elasticity of the muscles is optimized; the body is "loaded" with energy.

In the previous chapter "Thinking...Seeing...Feeling" we discussed the different ways we as humans learn new tasks, so, as a review, let's quickly analyze The Running Pose by those criteria. First, our thought process tells us that the Running Pose makes sense. The body is balanced, the body is compact, the body is ready to move. No energy is being wasted and the runner is relaxed, ready to direct all his or her energy to the simple task of moving forward.

Second, from a visualization standpoint, think of a cheetah flowing across a plain in pursuit of prey (Fig. 11.7). Use your mind to stop the action at the one point in the action where all four of the cheetah's feet are directly under the

Fig. 11.5 The ball on the edge of the table - ready to fall

58

body, where the incredible running muscles have all relaxed and where you know that the cheetah is just loaded with energy, set to explode into the next stride. That is the cheetah's Running Pose; the human Running Pose is just as loaded with energy, just as ready to explode.

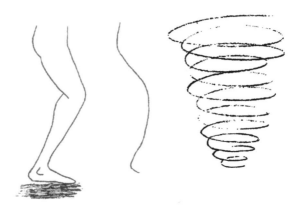

Fig. 11.6 S (spring) - like body position accumulates the muscles' elasticity energy, the ability

Fig. 11.7. Cheetah's run

59

And finally, how do we feel in the Running Pose? Centered. Balanced. Relaxed. If we haven't mastered the Running Pose, we make minute muscular contractions to the left and right, fore and aft, to hold the pose. That's wasted energy. When the pose has been perfected, we feel as if we could stand there all day, yet be ready to move forward, swiftly and effortlessly on a moment's notice.

Chapter 12

Here's good advice for practice;
go into partnership with nature,
she does more than half the work
and asks none of the fee.
Martin H. Fisher

THE FREE FALLING CONCEPT

As spectators, when we watch a great runner in action we tend to describe his or her running style as relaxed, free and effortless. In other words, we tend to regard a great runner as someone who moves with complete freedom of movement. While humans are by nature great imitators, it's funny that we don't try to imitate great runners in the same way that we might try to replicate the swing of a Tiger Woods or Barry Bonds or the shooting technique of a Michael Jordan. We may be envious of the great runner, but tend to regard that freedom of movement as a gift from nature and not a style to be copied.

And while we don't even try to emulate a perfect running style, we give even less thought to the source of that freedom of movement. If we were watching instead a magician, we would certainly ask, "how does he do it" but when we watch a runner float along seemingly impervious to gravity, we fail to ask the same question.

Interestingly enough, the answer is right there – gravity (Fig. 12.1). The great runner is not impervious to gravity; instead he taps it as a readily available source of free energy. In the same way that the tremendous force of gravity inevitably draws a free-falling skydiver toward Earth, we can appropriate the force of gravity to run further, faster and with less effort.

Gravity is with us 24 hours a day. It impacts every movement we make and indeed our relationship to gravity has impacted our physical development ever since we emerged from the womb. Yet despite the fact that we are constantly in the grasp of gravity, we devote almost no time to learning about it. For us, gravity simply exists, but we rarely think about our relationship with it. In fact, the role that gravity plays in human movement is so critical that you could say trying to run without understanding gravity is like trying to sail without understanding the wind.

To carry the analogy further, in the same way that a sailor catches the wind to move the boat forward (Fig. 12.2), we can "catch" the power of gravity to move our bodies forward (Fig. 12.3). It is the ultimate freedom of movement, taking a free and abundant energy source – gravity – and harnessing it to run like the wind. Remember, the boat doesn't use the force of the sailor to move forward; it is the skill of the sailor in capturing the force of the wind that moves the boat forward. In running, it will be your skill in transferring the force of gravity into horizontal movement that determines just how far and fast you can run.

Ironically, for all our obliviousness to the potential value of gravity in movement, the concept is not a new one. In the 15th century, none other than the original Renaissance man himself, Leonardo da Vinci, detailed the role of terrestrial attraction (gravity) in initiating movement. "Motion," Leonardo explained, "is created by the destruction of balance, that is, of equality of weight, for nothing can move by itself which does not leave its state of balance and that thing moves most rapidly which is furthest from its balance." Further, he added, "of the motion and course of animals, that figure will appear swiftest in its course which is about to fall forwards" (1). In other words, a free falling animal moves fastest.

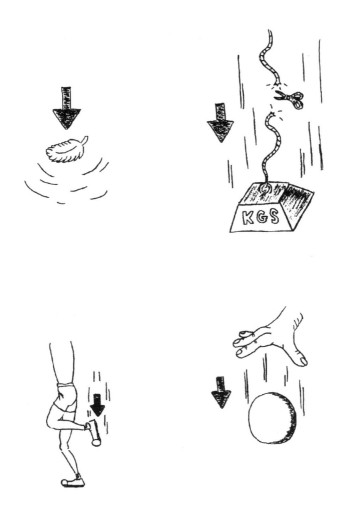

Fig. 12.1. "The work of gravity." Gravity force moves all bodies toward the Earth with constant acceleration of 9.8 m/sec²

Gravity being a constant force, nothing much has changed in our understanding of it since Leonardo's time. What can be changed, however, is the way we put that knowledge to use in a scientifically structured program to develop a superior running technique. To wit, in order to run better, we must teach our bodies to be free to fall. The degree to which we successfully assimilate this skill will be immediately apparent in both our speed and endurance. Simply put, superior running technique is the art of releasing the body to fall freely.

Fig. 12.2. The sail boat. The sailor does not move the boat, he moves the sails to catch the wind, which moves the boat

The challenge now lies in developing the logical process, the exact sequence of movements that will result in the greatest ability of the body to freely fall forward. As Leonardo demonstrated, the body preparing to fall should be in the greatest state of readiness to fall, meaning that it should be in a state of balance, but a very shaky state of balance. In this shaky state of balance it will take the least possible amount of energy to initiate the fall.

For us as runners, this precarious state of balance is achieved in what we call the Running Pose. The weight of the body is on the balls of the feet, the knees are slightly bent and the signal from the brain permitting the body to start falling is very easily accomplished, with minimal physical effort. As you can easily see for yourself, in order to initiate the fall from the Running Pose, all you have to do is relax your muscles and let your body fall forward while maintaining perfect lateral balance.

But you cannot fall while both feet are on the ground, so the second element of the fall is to create the situation by which the lead foot is also falling, which is done by removing it from support and lifting it into the air. This, in turn, can only be accomplished by yet a third, and most subtle, movement, that of lifting the body to a minimal height and then drawing the foot to *follow* the body.

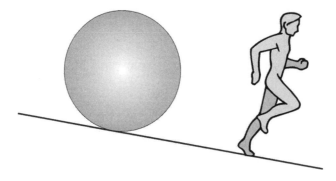

Fig. 12.3. "The downhill running by gravity pull"

This last movement, the lifting of the body, is not a bounce. It is merely the use of muscular elasticity to draw the body in an almost imperceptible way away from the ground. As you might imagine, all three of these actions occur simultaneously and are directed to transfer of support from one foot to the other. To an observer, the only motion that would be noticed in this precise sequence is the lifting of the foot directly under the pelvis, but what is really occurring is that the foot is following the much more subtle movements of the body to fall forward. This lifting of the foot from support is accomplished entirely by the hamstring.

In essence, the brain is giving the body three simultaneous commands to start the free falling process: 1) allow the fall;

2) move the body from support and 3) remove the foot from support. Of these, the first two are accomplished primarily on a subconscious level while the third, the lifting of the foot, is a much more conscious act and initiates and integrates the entire cycle of movements in the running stride.

Put simply, starting to run is as basic as falling forward.

1. Keele, K.D., 1983, Leonardo da Vinci's Elements of the Science of Man, New York, Academic Press, pp. 173-175.

Chapter 13

ALTERNATING POSES

Movement is Changing of Support

Fig. 13.1. Movement is a consequence of changing support

Here's where it all comes together and we see just how simple the Pose Method of Running really is. What do you think of when you think of running? Do words like pounding, lunging, pain and suffering come to mind? Do you conjure up images of your legs stretching ahead of you, your arms pumping furiously, your breath coming in short, labored

67

gasps as sweat pours out of your body?

Here's a new image for you. Running is simply the changing of support from one leg to the other. Simple as that. One instant, you are in the Running Pose supported on one leg, the next you are in the Running Pose supported on the other leg. Your only objective is to alternate your Running Poses from one leg to the other as quickly as possible. Running is what takes place in between. Running happens.

When you think about it, any movement you see around you, can be simply defined as a change of support from one point to the next. A car rolls forward as its support rotates from point to point on each of its four tires. A snake wriggles across the ground with surprising speed as it changes support from one point to the next along its continuous body. Even birds in the sky and fish in the sea simply change their points of support as they move forward in their respective media (Fig. 13.1).

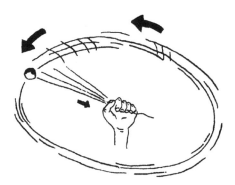

Fig. 13.2. The quick rotational movement is an instance of change of support

How fast a body moves is determined entirely by how quickly (Fig. 13.2) and efficiently (Fig. 13.3) it changes its support. Interestingly, the perfect change of support comes from the body's willingness to fall. Let's think about this for a moment. When a body is perfectly balanced, perfectly compact and perfectly ready to move, its movement starts when the balance is released. The body is now falling, moving forward at the speed of gravity. What prevents the body from striking the ground is the change of support from one leg to the next. The speed with which this change takes place, and balance is restored, mandates how fast the body moves forward through time and space. The faster the body changes support, the faster it moves. Or to think about it from the other direction, the longer support remains in a single place on the ground, the slower the body moves.

Fig. 13.3. "A different change of support"

Now let's translate this theory to the art of human running. Everything proceeds from the base position, the Running Pose. Remember, the runner is in the S-like stance, perfectly balanced, compact and loaded with energy. The act of running begins when the runner simply lifts his support foot from the ground, straight up under the pelvis (Fig. 13.4). All the muscular effort to remove the foot from the ground comes from the hamstring. The action of the hamstring initiates the release of the foot from the ground and sets up the direction of the shin and foot movement under the hip.

69

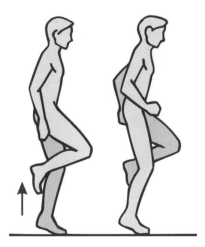

Fig. 13.4. Changing support by lifting the foot from the ground

What we think about is only the simple movement of picking the foot up off the ground. We don't think about unbending the support leg, because this movement is on the level of automatic control and performance. The mind sends out the signal "lift the foot straight up" and the leg automatically responds.

In the Running Pose, the body is maximally loaded with the energy of muscular resilience and is waiting for the command to unbend the joints. But we don't want to think about "unbending" for two reasons. First, we need to minimize the oscillation of our general center of mass – our body. In other words, we don't want to be bouncing up and down. The energy that it takes to lift our trunk, arms, shoulders and head is tremendous and utterly unnecessary for the task of moving the body forward. So, any thought of unbending (straightening) the leg might cause us to subconsciously try to move the body upwards.

Secondly, we don't want to think about trying to use the legs to move the body forward. Funny, but that's probably what you thought running really was – moving the body forward with the legs. Again, this would be a waste of energy as you subconsciously tried to drive yourself forward by unbending your leg to push off the ground and surge ahead.

Instead, all we need to do is pick the foot up under the body – nothing more. With respect to the ground, the vertical movement of the body should be minimized as much as possible. The feet move up and down under the body. The body itself remains as still as possible.

Let's go back to the analogy of a moving car. The cab of the car stays perfectly level as it moves forward down the road. Unless it hits a bump, the cab never moves up or down. All the propulsive action takes place below. In fact, the wheels are constantly rolling to keep up with the forward momentum of the cab.

Now, imagine the trunk of your body as the cab of the car. The action takes place underneath your pelvis, which itself remains still as it is propelled forward. To fully appreciate this requires a different mindset. Most runners measure their progress primarily by visual means and secondarily by the watch.

Visually, you pick out a point some distance down the road or trail and measure your progress by how quickly you close the gap between your current position and the chosen point. And, the watch, of course, gives you an absolute judgment on the time necessary to cover a given distance.

In both cases, the results are indicative of how *fast* you have run, but not on how *well* you have run. Your frame of reference is either a quick visual check or a result relative to your own previous efforts on the same course or distance. In either case, your mindset is to measure the results of your efforts, not the process of those efforts.

In order to reorient that mindset, focus on the lower trunk of your body as you run. Disregard the watch and the visual cues and feel your trunk, in all its stillness, moving forward. The trunk isn't doing any work, yet as the turnover rate of the legs beneath it gets faster and faster, you can actually feel the trunk accelerate. This is the feeling you're looking for – a complete disassociation between the body, which is being accelerated by gravity, and the legs, which are merely changing support at an increasing rate.

If this all sounds a bit Zen-like, that's okay. To maximize your potential as a runner, you have to minimize wasted effort and energy. The Pose Method of Running requires that you do only what is necessary to allow the body to move forward without falling, nothing more. It is a very precise orchestration of minimal movement, repeated very quickly, with complete focus.

The hamstring lifts the foot from the ground, the body begins to fall, the foot returns softly to the ground, and the body stays upright while moving forward. The faster you change support and alternate your poses, the faster you run. It's just that simple.

Chapter 14

Simplicity is the ultimate sophistication.
Leonardo da Vinci

THE WHEEL CONCEPT

Bicycles and cars roll right down the road, but what about runners? Given the analogies used in the past couple of chapters, it probably won't surprise you that the movement of the wheel is an ideal representation of the biomechanical essence of running. In chapter 13, we compared the torso of the body to the cab of a car, but we said virtually nothing about the wheels under the car. Here we go...

The wheel is one of the most perfect appliances in existence (2). Despite its apparent simplicity, the wheel is a complex mechanism with three mechanical properties that have significant implications for human movement (Fig.14.1). First, the wheel is mechanically effective, in that it facilitates forward movement with minimal vertical oscillation. This was noted in the chapter on alternating poses, where we discussed the fact that the cab of a car remains still while the car itself moves forward.

Fig. 14.1. The wheel's mechanical properties of efficient movement

The second significant property is the relationship between the support point of the wheel and the body (General Center of Mass or GCM) it is moving. During the entire cycle of a wheel, the distance between the support and the body it is moving never changes. Similarly, the relative position of the two also remains constant.

The final critical detail is that the point of support is constantly changing, no matter what the forward speed of the wheel might be. Further, the forward speed of the body being moved is exactly proportionate to the

Fig. 14.2. "Unicyclist riding." The movement happens when the unicyclist leans towards desirable direction

74

speed at which the support point is changed.

To give a visual representation of these mechanical properties, let's simplify our car analogy a little bit and think of a person riding a unicycle (Fig. 14.2). In this analogy, the "body" is both the frame and saddle of the unicycle and the rider perched on it. Underneath is a perfect moving circumference, the wheel. At any point in the rotation of the wheel only one point on the wheel is in contact with the ground. This is the support point, upon which rests all the weight of the body.

Reflecting the first critical mechanical point, as the unicycle rolls down the road, the wheel is turning, changing support points, but there is no vertical oscillation. The rider's head remains perfectly level. Why is this important?

As they say on TV, let's go to the tape, specifically the broadcast of the 1981 New York City Marathon. As Tim Noakes explained in his 1991 book, "The Lore of Running"(3), the broadcast included a dramatic sequence of Alberto Salazar, then the world's top marathoner, as he crossed the Queensborough Bridge. In the angle shown on TV, only Salazar's head and shoulders were visible above the bridge wall and it was clear that his head was remaining absolutely parallel to the top of the wall. In other words, there was no vertical oscillation created by his stride, no energy wasted in lifting and lowering the body. The "Salazar Shuffle" was indeed an efficient means of forward locomotion.

Going back to the unicycle, we note also that as the wheel rolls forward, neither the distance between the point of support and the rider nor their spatial relationship changes. The point of support is always directly beneath the saddle, the torso and ultimately the head of the rider. This relationship is the most efficient for retaining forward motion in the horizontal plane, minimizing any potential braking effects.

Going further, we can look at the rider's feet as the pedaling motion goes through its cycle. Whenever a foot is at the bottom of the pedal stroke, where is it? Directly beneath the rider's torso, with the leg slightly bent. Remove the unicycle from your mental image and what do you have? A runner in the Running Pose, both legs bent, support on the ball of the foot with the body in a straight line above the point of support. Landing with all the weight of the body directly above the point of support on a leg, that is bent to minimize shock, substantially decreases the load on muscles, ligaments and joints and thus decreases the chance of sustaining injury.

Now put the rider back on the unicycle to consider the final critical mechanical property of the wheel: the proportional relationship between the speed at which the point of support is changed and the speed with which the body moves forward. Very simply, the faster support is changed, the faster the body moves. The lesson here is that the faster a runner's stride, i.e. the faster he changes support from one foot to the next, the faster his forward speed will be. Stride frequency, not length, is the key to faster running.

It is true that while the wheel constantly changes support from one point to the next, the human can't duplicate this exact biomechanical efficiency, given only two feet to trade the support. However, we can approach the feeling of uninterrupted change of support. The faster we change support, the more we can visualize our legs as a wheel. We can indeed roll down the road, just as we suggested at the top of this chapter.

Confirmation of this comes from practical studies that demonstrate that elite runners have a faster stride rate than run-of-the-mill athletes at all distances. In his 1997 book Daniels' Running Formula, the respected American coach Jack Daniels noted that there is data from his many years of practical observation that indicates elite runners tend to run with a stride frequency of not less than 180 strides per minute, which he links to good technique (1).

If you look at this statistic "backwards", i.e. first noting that elite runners run with high stride rates, the critical importance of perfect form and efficiency becomes obvious. It is simply impossible to maintain such a high stride rate over any significant distance with poor form. There's a common phrase race commentators use when the form of a competitive runner begins to deteriorate in the latter stages of a race and it couldn't ring any truer. "It looks like the wheels have come off," they say, and when you look at the runner, you know exactly what they mean. The form and efficiency are gone and the runner is now struggling to finish, no longer a contender for victory.

The meaning of the wheel concept is really very simple: to move with wheel-like efficiency, we must minimize bounce (vertical oscillation), land with support directly under the body and maintain a high stride rate. The Pose Method of Running is designed to accomplish all three of these goals.

1. Daniels, J., Daniels' Running Formula, Champaign, IL, Human Kinetics, pp. 80-82.
2. Margaria, R., 1976, Biomechanics and Energetics of Muscular Exercise, Oxford, Oxford University Press, pp. 105-108.
3. Noakes, T., 1991, Lore of Running. Discover the science and spirit of running, Champaign, IL, Leisure Press, p. 29.

Chapter 15

Come forth into the light of things;
let nature be your teacher.
William Wordsworth

MUSCULAR ELASTICITY

Cars, unicycles…what comes next in our efforts to reveal the underlying nature of pure running form? Actually, we find out next role models in nature, as we study the running form of dogs, cats and other swift animals. The S-like stance of the Running Pose was conceived to emulate the rear legs of animals who can run both fast and far (Fig. 15.1). Look at the accompanying photos demonstrating a variety of animals at speed. In each case, the rear legs are bent in all joints. There is no full extension, no complete unbending in the joints. This is completely natural running. And it merits further study to understand its implications for human movement.

The principal asset of the S-like stance is that it facilitates optimum muscular elasticity. Elasticity is the ability of muscles to perform work, specifically to contract rapidly after an immediately prior extension. Nature's design for running, the S-like stance, keeps all the connective tissue – muscles, tendons and ligaments – in

Fig. 15.1. Rear legs of animals have S-like shape

a resilient, elastic state (Fig. 15.2). Connective tissue that is not stretched to the limit remains supple and able to work efficiently. Here's a test you can perform at home with a dog or cat. First, try to stretch one of their rear legs to a fully straightened position. It's virtually impossible. Nature has designed these legs to remain bent, keeping everything nice and relaxed. Then, dig your fingertips into the thigh muscle of the animal. You might expect to feel a very hard muscle and be growled at by animal in pain. Instead you'll receive an impassive stare and feel very pliable muscle tissue. You can actually press all the way to the bone without causing any discomfort to the animal whatsoever.

It's funny, but we are conditioned by the media to think of "rock-hard" muscles as representing the ultimate in strength when in fact the opposite is true. The muscle that is the supplest and most elastic is the one capable of performing efficient work. Conversely, a rock hard muscle is laced with scar tissue and is too stiff to work efficiently. Among other things, this explains the importance of massage and stretching as a component of a complete training regimen. Keeping your muscles pliable and injury-free will be a major component in determining your level of success in running.

While we still have the dog or cat around, we can take note of yet another feature of nature's running design – no heels. Dogs, cats and other animals don't strike the ground with their heels because they don't have them. Natural selection has forced them to run on the front part of the foot.

In the same fashion, in the Running Pose the runner is supported on the ball of the foot, with the leg bent in all joints (especially the knee joint) and the heel slightly above the support (or even lightly touching it.) Most important, the weight is always kept on the ball of the foot. The Running Pose is lifted directly from nature and maintains all the connective tissue in a state of optimal preparedness to perform efficient work.

Fig. 15.2. "The work of elasticity"

While running, you must always remain is this pose as you change support from one foot to the next. By faithfully staying in the pose you maximize the use of your muscular elasticity and resilience and thus reduce your energy expenditures. In fact, a 1964 study (2) indicated that mechanical efficiency of running increased up to 50%, due to contributions from elastic storage and return of energy…

81

The payoff to "elastic" running is that you can maintain a high stride rate without "going anaerobic" and using up your body's available energy supply of ATP (adrenotriphosphate), the fuel of your highest intensity sprints. Elastic running gives you the ability to run faster for greater distances and still keep something in reserve (1, 3 & 4).

With the obvious benefits of elastic running, you may be tempted to bound right out the front door and begin running at stride rates of 180 or even greater. It might be better to temper that enthusiasm and not get ahead of yourself. The first element of running elastically is to master the Pose Method of Running. You must coordinate your muscles into an integral system of running to the point where it feels absolutely natural. That alone takes time and complete focus and you are well advised to concentrate your initial Pose Running efforts entirely on tecnique.

Significantly, though, the second element of elastic running is to develop the strength of your muscle systems so that you are able to quicken your movements and reduce the amount of time you actually spend on support. The faster you pick your foot off the ground, the faster you will run. While it is true that running itself does develop some of the strength necessary to quicken these movements, the fact is that specialized strength training will be required to fully take advantage of your newly refined Pose Running style. All the special exercises necessary to enhance your muscular strength will be covered in Section Five "Building A Runner's Body...and Mind."

1. Alexander, A.M., 1988, Springs as energy stores: running. Elastic mechanisms in animal movement. Cambridge, Cambridge University Press, pp. 31-50.
2. Cavagna, G.A., Saibene, F.P. and Margaria, R., 1964, Mechanical work in running, J. Appl. Physiol., 19:249-256
3. Cavagna, G.A., 1977, Storage and utilization of elastic energy in skeletal muscle. Exercise and Sport Science Reviews, 5, 89-129.
4. Cavagna, P.R., La Fortune M.A., 1980, Ground reaction forces in distance running, J. Biomech, 13:397-406.

Chapter 16

Top runners have quick turnover.
Jack Daniels

THE IMPORTANCE OF RAPID STRIDE FREQUENCY

Why is stride frequency so important? Why do we pay so much attention to this single running parameter? Why do we focus on cadence and not stride length? Don't we cover more ground with a longer stride and therefore run faster? When it comes down to actually considering what our legs do when we run, there are a lot of valid questions. Fortunately, as usual, the answers lie in simplicity, albeit a somewhat complicated simplicity.

The frequency of our strides in running is really nothing more than the rate at which we change support from one foot to the next, which is the essence of good running technique. When we change support, we start free falling and let the force of gravity accelerate us forward. The faster we change support, the less we do to interrupt the gravitational pull and the faster we run. It really is that simple.

83

Conversely, if we attempt to run with a longer stride, we slow down. Why? Again, the answer is simple. In order to lengthen the stride, we thrust the leg out in front of the body. As soon as the leading foot strikes the ground, it is planted there until the entire body passes over it. So, instead of changing support very quickly, the long stride means that it changes very slowly, which interrupts the pull of gravity and slows the forward progress of the body.

Here's a little test to prove the concept. Get dressed for a run and then warm-up thoroughly. Once you're good to go, pick a little straight stretch of road and select a 'finish line' about 40 yards away. Sprint with all you've got and then stop after you pass over your finish line.

Here's what happened: after you passed your finish line and began to stop, your stride actually lengthened. Subconsciously, you sent out the 'slow down' signal to your body, which responded by lengthening the

Fig. 16.1 "Knee overloading"

stride to put a braking effect on your forward momentum. In other words, the body knew that the quickest way to slow down was to put the brakes on the pull of gravity. As it slowed you down, it also put tremendous force on your quads and knees (Fig. 16.1). It actually took more energy to stop than it would to have kept moving forward.

There are many lessons we can take from this. Most important is the simple notion that the less we do to counteract the force of gravity, the faster we run. Inherent in that concept is the fact that the less time we spend with a foot on the ground, the less we do to counteract gravity. Even better, the less we do to counteract gravity, the less load we place on joints, ligaments and tendons, which in turn reduces our chance of injury.

84

Whether we run fast or slow, we still benefit from using our muscular elasticity to reduce tension and run with a light touch, instead of pounding it out as we would with a longer stride. What makes increased stride frequency critical, though, is that it is the only parameter of running speed that we can consciously control.

Acceleration due to gravity is a constant, but our ability to take full advantage of gravity's pull is a function of our body lean and our stride cadence. To put it in basic terms, if you lean forward and don't move your foot to create a new point of support, you will quickly find yourself face first on the ground. Lean very slightly and you can move your foot slowly to prevent hitting the ground. You're still falling forward – you're just not falling down. Lean more and you have to move your feet faster to avoid hitting the ground with your face.

This is the essence of the symbiotic relationship between stride frequency and body lean. The faster you change support, the more permission you give to your body to freefall. And the faster you fall, the faster you run. Your running speed is directly related to your stride frequency or cadence.

Don't believe it? Watch any high caliber running race and even to an untrained eye it will be obvious that the difference between elite runners and merely good runners, indeed the difference between winners and losers, is stride frequency (Fig. 16.2).

It is critical to bear in mind that a high stride frequency

Fig. 16.2. "Running with high frequency"

85

does not demand a huge muscular effort. On the contrary, you should do everything in your power to avoid unnecessary effort and tension. Concentrate and use your muscular elasticity to pull your foot just off the ground, making only the effort necessary to break the point of contact between foot and ground. Focus your efforts on carefully synchronizing your increased stride frequency with the rate at which your body is falling forward and you will soon be running faster...and further... than you would ever have imagined.

Chapter 17

*In anything at all,
perfection is finally attained
not when there is no longer
anything left to add,
but when there is no longer
anything to take away.*
Antoine de Saint-Exupery

DON'T JUST RUN: DO NOTHING!

To this point, we've discussed the many things you have to do to achieve the Running Pose and move yourself down the road or trail with the greatest possible efficiency. And, in truth, it's quite a lot to think about. You've got to keep all your joints bent, constantly fall forward, land on the balls of your feet, pick your foot off the ground as rapidly as possible, keep your trunk very still, focus on a rapid stride rate, etc.

With all that in mind, it may be comforting to know there are a lot of things that you don't do in the Pose Method of Running and that not doing the wrong things is as vital to your success as doing the right things. Comforting, but not necessarily easy.

87

What I call the "Do Nothing" concept was inspired by a session I conducted in June of 1996 at the USA Triathlon Junior Development Camp in Gainesville, Fla. As I worked with a group of junior triathletes, Stuart Newby Fraser, brother of the seven-time Ironman Hawaii champ Paula Newby Fraser, observed from the sidelines. After the junior session ended, Stuart approached me, interested in finding out for himself what this "Pose Method" was all about.

As soon as our session began, Stuart's frustration was obvious. No matter what he did, I was there with a correction, "Don't do this, don't do that." It seemed that no matter what I said, the first word was always "don't." Finally Stuart, completely exasperated, stopped, looked right at me and asked, "Nick, are you actually asking me to do nothing?"

Once I stopped laughing, I could only say, "Yes, Stuart, do nothing." Then I thanked him for giving a name to one of the most important principles of the Pose Method of Running – the "Do Nothing" concept.

Most runners, triathletes and other active sports enthusiasts are highly motivated people, the kind we've come to call Type 'A' personalities. Such people are action takers and always believe that there is something more they can do to make their efforts better. In the case of the Pose Method of Running, there is something more you can do – nothing! Which, of course isn't as easy as you might think.

Programmed to give every last measure to achieve top performance, it's not so easy for some of us to realize that top performance only comes when extraneous activities are eliminated. To run our best, we have to minimize everything that doesn't specifically contribute to moving the body forward against all the forces that are aligned against it.

In the Pose Method of Running, the key is to let things happen, not try to make them happen. Remember, gravity is a greater force than anything we can generate on our own, so we must learn to get out of the way and let gravity propel us forward while we preserve as much of our energy as possible for the simple act of picking our feet off the ground.

So, in order to "do nothing' there are a lot of "don'ts" involved.

Perhaps the toughest "don't" to master is this: **don't put your foot back on the ground** after you lift it (Fig. 17.1.a). Let gravity do the work of returning your foot to support. What this means is that as soon as you have used your hamstring to lift the foot from the ground, you must completely relax the leg and "let" it fall softly back to the ground. Doing this will synchronize the return of the foot to support with the passage of your body over that spot, meaning that your footfall will be exactly where it is supposed to be, in line with your trunk, neck and head.

Fig. 17.1. Don't do it:
a. The foot is forcefully moved down.
b. The knee is lifted up and driven forward.
c. The rear leg is extended to push the body off the ground.

Conversely, if you force your foot back down, a number of things can happen, all of them bad. First, your natural rhythm will be destroyed and you will be completely out of sync in your stride pattern. Your foot will land ahead of you and absorb the impact of your weight as your body passes over the point of support. That, plus the actual impact caused by the force you have applied in pushing the foot down, will greatly increase your chance of injury. And, finally, by pushing your foot down, you needlessly expend energy that could be used for the far more important task of lifting the foot back up.

It will take a great deal of concentration to allow your foot to "free fall," but doing so is key to mastering the Pose technique.

Just as important, **don't lift or drive forward with your knees and hips** (Fig. 17.1.b). Again, this is a tremendous waste of energy. Your upper legs are heavy, and lifting them 180 times a minute is a brutal exercise, totally unnecessary for the job of moving your body forward.

Remember the only thing you have to do to free your body is to lift your support foot directly under the pelvis. The only muscle required to do this is the big ol' hamstring, which is ideally suited to the task. Bringing the calves, the quads and other muscle groups into the equation burns energy and fatigues the body. Further, driving forward with this part of your leg means that at some point it is going to have to wait while the rest of the body catches up. This is a waste of time. Don't do it.

Similarly, unbending your knee joint (straightening your leg) creates havoc with your running technique. **Don't straighten your leg** (Fig. 17.1.c). First, this accelerates your shin toward the ground, in front of your body, which creates an awful impact as the foot, now needlessly out in front of the body, absorbs all of your weight multiplied by the velocity at which you are traveling. This nasty blow is made worse by the fact that your leg is now straight, with no way to cushion the shock of all that energy and mass. It's too painful to think about. Ever had shin splints? No? Just straighten your legs while you run and experience that lovely sensation…and spend weeks hobbling around.

If the shin splints aren't bad enough, the other problem with straightening your leg is even worse – slower running. Think about it. You've straightened your leg and accelerated it forward. Sound familiar? Right. It's now out in front of your body, playing the old waiting game. Instead of your foot being quickly removed from support to start the next cycle, it's now firmly planted on the ground, waiting for you to catch up. The longer it's stuck to the ground, the greater the braking force, the slower you move forward. Let's repeat – **don't straighten your leg**.

Fig. 17.2. "Don't drive with your arms"

Don't drive with your arms (Fig. 17.2). You're not carrying a football toward the end zone, trying to shed tacklers; you're trying to move smoothly down the road. The main function of your arms is not to drive the body forward but to provide balance and equilibrium as gravity pulls you forward. As your hamstrings do all the work, there is an easy, natural, rhythmic flow to your arms that provides the balance that keeps you comfortably in stride, but nothing more. Don't force the issue. Let your arms and hands remain relaxed while you conserve energy and move forward.

While the Do Nothing concept may not be as easy as it sounds, it's sure a lot better than the alternative, which is running slower and creating unnecessary injuries. Sometimes the most important part of doing something right is to not do everything wrong. That's certainly the case with running, where it's doing the wrong things that can kill you. It takes a lot of mental focus to do only that which is necessary and let everything else be relaxed, but that's exactly what it takes to run further and faster.

Chapter 18

*There is a time and
a place for everything.*
Proverb

THE FRAMING CONCEPT
(AKA Running In The Space-Time Continuum)

What is running, really? While it may seem a bit odd to be raising such a question this far into a book on running technique, it's certain that your answer will be different now than it would have been at page one. So, let's give it a go and try to define this basic human activity that still enthralls us.

Basically, running is the act of moving a piece of cargo down the road or trail using the force of gravity and the power of muscular contractions. That cargo, of course, is your body, the very thing you have been carting around your entire life. In that sense, you've been moving that cargo through space and time, wherever you have roamed and however long you've been living.

Now, through running, you're attempting to move that cargo across a predetermined amount of space in the minimum possible amount of time. Timing, in running as it is in life, is everything.

Throughout your life, how many times have you thought to yourself, "I was born ten years too late?" How many times have you been too late to a meeting or undertaken a task before you were ready for it? Have you had a marriage that went bad because you married too young? Or maybe you lost a big contract because you were tied up in traffic and were late to a meeting.

The consequences of poor timing can be catastrophic...or they can be minor annoyances quickly forgotten. No matter what the case, whenever you can control timing, it works to your advantage. So it is when you run.

In this case, timing doesn't refer to the amount of time it takes you to complete a given distance, but to the closely synchronized movements of your body as it moves through space and time. We have discussed many critical elements of the Pose Method of Running, ranging from the S-shaped position of the body, the always bent position of the joints, the foot strike on the balls of the feet and the importance of minimizing extraneous energy expenditures, just to name a few. Now is the time to discuss timing.

As we have seen, running is not simply the passage of the body over a given expanse of terrain; it is also the repetition of a set of poses designed to efficiently and quickly change support from one foot to the next. For the highest level of running, you must repeat these poses as perfectly as possible, as quickly as possible. Most importantly, they must be repeated with precise coordination, with every pose being synchronized with the movement of the body in space.

To give a visual picture to this, imagine that a movie camera tracks alongside you as you run down a rolling trail. The lens frames you so that your head is at the top of the frame and the ground forms the bottom of the frame. The two sides of the frame are closely cropped on either side of your body.

A movie camera exposes 24 frames per second, so when you examine the film frame-by-frame, you have an excellent visual representation of your running style. Since the camera never lies, it helps to know how to evaluate the film. The first thing to understand is that any time any part of your body leaves the frame of the picture, you've done something wrong.

Fig. 18.1. "Holding the support foot on the ground too long"

For example, if the "swing" foot (the one that is in the air) moves out of the frame to the back (behind you), then what happened is that it remained on the ground too long, rather than being pulled up immediately under the hip joint. While that foot was stuck to the ground, the body moved on past it, resulting in a foot trailing the body (Fig. 18.1). Now the trailing foot is engaged in a game of catch-up, requiring other muscles to come to the rescue and bring the foot forward. In turn, this increases the energy expenditure and results in increased fatigue. Ironically, you're now both working harder and running slower. Slower, because the foot stayed too long on the ground and harder because of the extra work being performed. Bad timing leads to poor performance.

Conversely, if the "swing" foot goes out the front of the frame, then it has been straightened and pushed forward (Fig. 18.2). Again the timing is destroyed and poor performance is the result. First, by being in front of the body, the foot causes a braking effect. There is no way to lift the foot until the body is over the foot, so there is no forward progress while the body is in catch-up mode. Worse, by being in front of the body, the leg absorbs the full impact of the body's weight, greatly increasing the risk of injury.

Fig. 18.2. "Swinging the leg out of the frame"
One brakes the flow of the body movement by throwing the leg too far ahead of the body

Section IV

MOVING FROM THOUGHT TO ACTION

Chapter 19

I never saw a Moor,
I never saw the Sea,
Yet know I how the Heather looks
And what a Willow be.
Emily Dickinson

INTEGRATING THE COMPONENTS OF THE POSE METHOD INTO YOUR NEW RUNNING STYLE

For something that is based on pure simplicity, the Pose Method can at times seem quite overwhelming. "I used to just step out the door and go running", you might say to yourself, "now I've got to worry about staying in frame, falling forward, acting like a wheel, I even have to think about doing nothing."

Yes, there are a lot of concepts, science and thought involved in perfecting the Pose Method of Running, but here's the key: they all say the same thing. Every concept that has been articulated in this book to this point is just another way of helping you to develop the proper mindset to run in the Pose Method. If you understand why something works, you'll be much more likely to make the commitment to devote yourself to learning it.

Now we've reached the point to move from a philosophical acceptance of the Pose Method to actually mastering the physical movements that comprise Pose Running. The first step is to experience the physical sensations that are part and parcel of Pose Running.

Consider weightlessness for a moment, if you will. Since the dawn of space travel, most of us have had an intellectual grasp of what weightlessness is, but few of us have ever actually experienced the sensation, save for a fleeting moment at the top of a roller coaster ride or in a stunt plane. But for those relatively few astronauts and cosmonauts who have experienced true weightlessness in outer space, there was a long road and lots of commitment to get there.

Similarly, we can now believe we know what the Pose Method is supposed to feel like, but in all likelihood we'll head out the door with all these concepts spinning through our heads and clunk down the road like we always did, saying to ourselves, "Is this it? Is this the Pose Method?"

And of course it won't be the Pose Method. So, to get you from where you are now, which is intellectually grasping the concepts of the Pose Method, to where you want to be, which is effortlessly floating down the road Pose-style, will also require a long road and a lot of commitment.

Just as you might have had a taste of weightlessness on a roller coaster, you have to grab that initial physical sensation of the Pose Method and experience the "A-ha!" moment, when what you are doing truly feels different from the way you have run before. After you get a sense of what it feels like to run with gravity providing the energy, it will become easier and easier for you to fine-tune the style and become a true Pose runner.

Of course, this is not a process left to chance. The next two sections of the book are devoted to transitioning from the intellectual to the physical. Again and again, you will perform drills that help you to unleash the force of gravity through your muscular

100

system to propel you down the road. And weightlessness, of a sort, is a key component of what you will experience. Properly channel your actions and you will run with a lighter, faster touch than ever before.

As you progress through these drills, you must always keep in mind that they are all designed to reinforce the same physical sensations. What you will do is come to the gradual realization that all the concepts are integrated. You can't increase your forward lean to increase velocity without reducing the time your feet remain on support. And if you don't increase your cadence to keep up, then your legs will fall behind your body, you'll move out of your frame and the result will be a total loss of form.

That's why the initial phase of learning the Pose Method depends so much on technique with so little emphasis on mileage. At this stage it is vital to be utterly precise in your movements. Any time you lose the critical coordination that integrates the concepts of the Pose Method, you have to stop, rest, gather your thoughts and try again. The last thing you want to do is let some sense of guilt urge you to rack up miles, if you can't retain your form while doing so.

Then, after you're confident that you have mastered the physical elements of the Pose Method, you'll move on to a set of drills that are oriented to developing the specific physical strength necessary to maintain the Pose form over greater and greater distances. Specific drills will enhance your muscular elasticity, develop strength in the hips and hamstrings and train your entire body to hold form as you run faster and faster, further and further.

And through this entire process, it must be said again, you'll be learning the same concepts over and over, integrating them into a system of movements designed to free gravity to pull you forward. To emphasize the connection between specific drills and the Pose Method, you must always run 15 to 20 steps after you perform every drill. Alternating between the drills and running gives you immediate feedback, making obvious in the physical sense what previously has only been an intellectual concept.

You will be sorely tempted to skip over these drills and "just run" from time to time. While the thought is very appealing, it would be akin to just taking a car out for a spin before you learn how to steer, brake and accelerate. Do yourself a favor and really get the feeling of the Pose Method before you take your body out for a long spin. Do the drills, then let gravity take over.

Chapter 20

*Practice and thought might
gradually forge many an art.*
Virgil

MASTERING RUNNING TECHNIQUE

For many of us, it is difficult to equate learning to run with more esoteric pursuits such as becoming a classical pianist or a ballet dancer. Running somehow seems like a more fundamental human activity while piano or dance appear to be more complex and artistic. Indeed, it is common to think of "running" as something "we do" while dance and piano are something "we learn."

The fact that we can run without specific instruction may be our biggest stumbling block toward learning to run properly. After all, we've all grown up progressing from crawling to walking to running, and we indisputably move faster when we run than when we walk. In that sense, it seems our running is successful. By contrast, anyone can pound on the keys, but it quite obvious to everyone that such pounding does not equate to making music. The same can be said for dance, where the difference between a skilled dancer and an ordinary klutz is painfully obvious.

So this seemingly natural and universal ability of humans to run has to a great extent obscured the fact that there is a talent or skill to run properly. In fact, like any other movement, the act of running is a skill that can be refined, trained and improved. Running technique is not unique to each individual human and it is more than just a series of properly performed movements. Just as is the case with classical piano or dance, running is the expression of all the physical, physiological, psychological, emotional, mental and spiritual qualities of an individual.

The Greeks, those masters of thought, gave us the word "technique", from the root word "techne", which means "art" or "mastery". Thus, when we are talking about the technique of some physical movement, we speak specifically of the art of performing this movement. And movements performed by humans do not exist independently. As human activity, they carry with them everything that being human implies, including all the mental, physical and spiritual make-up of the given human performing the activity.

As we live and learn, we master countless physical movements, which we routinely perform without a second thought. However the ease with which we perform those movements can be greatly affected by outside forces. Take the simple act of signing your name. Most of us have imbued our signature with a certain personal artistic flair and can sign automatically time after time. However, when we face a particularly important signature, such as a long-term mortgage or marriage certificate, our emotions can cause us to tense up and write very erratically.

Similarly, a classic pianist can perform flawlessly in rehearsal, but freeze up in front of an audience; a basketball player can sink 100 free throws in a row, but miss the one that could win the championship; and an ice skater can nail the quad in practice but blow it in the Olympics. In all these cases, and countless more, it is clear that mastery of movements, of technique, is more than just performing physical tasks by rote.

Movement technique, no matter the endeavor, is really a gate through which we channel all the characteristics that make us human. We communicate not just our physical abilities, but also our mental, psychological and spiritual components through every move we make. The pianist may make the physical keystrokes to create noise on the piano, but it is his or her mastery of piano technique on all levels that allows the expression of both the composer's and the pianist's understanding of the music.

While running is not as obviously creative as music, it too is an outlet for human expression and requires well-honed technique beyond the physical realm. Just as with dance, there is a rhythm and a beauty to running that transcends mere pavement pounding and elevates the act of running well to artistry.

As such, when we speak of mastering running technique, our objective is not just the mechanical repetition of free falling, changing support and staying within the running frame, but more importantly mastering all the components associated with *performance*. Yes, we have to first master the fundamentals of Pose Running and develop biomechanical capabilities of strength, speed and flexibility, but just as importantly we have to enhance our mental grasp of the formation of the movements, improve our space/time muscular sensitivity and build a psychological and spiritual profile that will equip us to run at the highest possible level.

Chapter 21

All our knowledge has its origin
in our perceptions.
Leonardo da Vinci

RUNNING SENSIBILITY

It is certainly no overstatement to say that most of us in modern society suffer from sensory overload these days. With oceans of signals and information washing over us from every angle, all the input tends to merge into a storm of white noise. It's a miracle if we can tend to day-to-day affairs, much less take on new initiatives. And learning to run is particularly vexing because, as we have discussed, most of us already think we know how to run.

Thus, we must both "unlearn" and learn at the same time, which requires the utmost attention to every vital piece of information put out by our bodies. We have to develop our ability to recognize these signals, "read" them and use that feedback to build a proper structure for our running movement.

Let's return for a moment to the discussion of the previous chapter where we compared learning to run to learning to play classical piano. When a musician is playing the piano, his or her skills directly depend on personal sensitivity in hearing, music tone, rhythm, etc., which have to be developed to an extraordinary level and then translated into the performance. In a sense, the pianist shuts out the outside world and develops a protective bubble occupied only by music.

As runners, we must develop the same heightened level of sensitivity to our movements. Typically, runners' senses exist in an eclectic, non-structured state in which some of the most vital senses are completely undeveloped. To put it bluntly, runners tend to hone in on a couple of things, mainly how fast they are going and how much they hurt and otherwise focus their thoughts elsewhere.

It is rare indeed for an unschooled runner to focus thoughts on more high-level sensations related to specific physical movements. However, to truly appreciate what we are doing as runners, we must identify these sensations and then develop them to a heightened state. The two most important sensations are gravity and free falling, but to develop them, we have to "tune in" to other feedback: the contact of our feet with the ground, a feeling of effortlessness, shortened time on support, and an overall sensation of lightness.

Going back to the concept of framing, what we do is create a mental bubble that corresponds to the physical frame within which we run. In this mental bubble, we focus only on the sensations that contribute toward perfect running technique, shutting out outside influences and heightening our sensitivity to our movements.

From a practical standpoint, it is probably wise to do a lot of your earlier Pose Method running either alone or with a mentor who is completely knowledgeable about the Pose Method. Otherwise, running socially with a friend will draw you out of your bubble and lead you away from concentration on developing these sensitivities. You may have a fun run, but as you either veer into conversation or begin trying to match your pace to your companion's, you'll lose the necessary focus on developing your skills.

As you get more and more skilled in developing your running sensibility, you'll become more sensitive to critical sensations like muscular elasticity, effortless increase of cadence and an overall sense of flow in your movement. One of the most telling signs in your development is that you will begin to regard your chest as something of an accelerator pedal: you'll realize that all you have to do to increase your speed is push forward from the solar plexus, increasing the angle of your forward lean, and you will automatically begin running faster. Pull back with your chest and your tempo will slow down.

By developing a finely honed running sensibility, you will appreciate just how the entire concept of "running" spans the gamut from physical movement to mental transportation. Just as a superb pianist's hands seem – even to the pianist himself – to be flowing across the keyboard as an autonomous entity, you will eventually find yourself flowing down the road or trail, with all your senses so perfectly melded that you are not even aware of your own heightened state of concentration. At that point, you are truly a runner, pure and simple.

Chapter 22

Learning without thought is labor lost;
Thought without learning is perilous.
Confucius

LEARNING THE RUNNING POSE

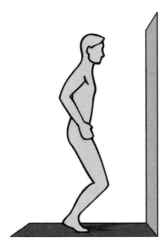

Fig. 22.1. Pose in front of the mirror (two feet position)

Now it's time to translate thought and theory into action. No, we're not going out for a fast 10K run, we're going to stand in front of a mirror and learn to run – without moving forward.

As we discussed in the last chapter, a body can only maximize its energy when no energy is being wasted. So the process of running that fast 10K begins by learning to be entirely comfortable and relaxed in the Running Pose.

Start by removing your shoes and standing in front of a full-length mirror. Both of your legs should be

111

slightly bent into an S-like stance (Fig. 22.1) Make sure that all your joints are bent and that you feel some slight tension in your muscles.

Lightly bounce in this position up and down without straightening your joints until you find the most comfortable angle for your legs. Don't lose contact with the ground, just weigh and unweigh your upper body as your legs seek the most comfortable position. Check the sensations in your feet and make sure your weight is on the balls of feet and not on either the toes or the heel (Fig. 22.2). This is critical

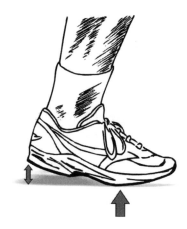

Fig. 22.2. "Placing the body weight on the ball of the foot"

– throughout the entire running cycle, your weight will only land on the balls of your feet and you must learn to really feel this sensation.

Now begin to skip in place in this S-like stance on both legs. Don't straighten your legs; barely lift them from the ground. Perform this movement softly. Try to sense the wholeness of your body's movements. Feel the elasticity of your muscles, not the unbending efforts in your joints.

As soon as one leg touches the ground, lightly and quickly reverse the movement of the body upwards. This reversal of the body movement up and down should be done with minimal effort and without ever stopping the movement. The objective is to transform the energy of the fall into the resilient deformation of the muscles and back. All your efforts are directed only to retaining the pose. Think of it this way, at the very instant your weight lands one foot you begin the process of getting your weight off that foot.
The best visual image is probably a bouncing ball (Fig. 22.3).

When a ball strikes the ground, you know that its outer surface flattens at the point of contact. But you also know that this compression signals the immediate equal and opposite reaction: the ball begins to spring back of the ground instantly. Similarly, as soon as you feel the ball off your foot touching the ground, the only thing you want to do is get it back off the ground.

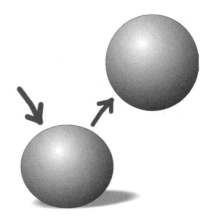

Fig. 22.3. A bouncing ball

While you "see" a bouncing ball, what you "feel" would be hot coals. As you're making these light skipping movements, imagine that every time your foot touches down it has just touched a blazing white-hot coal. Your reaction will be swift and purposeful.

Now you're ready to assume the Running Pose. Let's put it all together. Stand in place with the ball of one foot on the ground. The heel of that foot is barely off the ground and may even lightly contact the ground. Your body has assumed the S-like shape and your leg and trunk muscles are lightly tensed. Your non-support leg is barely off the ground, bent only slightly more than the support leg.

Hold your balance in this pose, with as little strain in your muscles as possible. If you have difficulty at first, use additional support from the wall, a chair or a willing partner. Once you begin to feel comfortable in the Running Pose, make some light, springing bounces. What you want to feel is the elasticity of your muscles, not their effort. Your body should feel like an integrated spring-like system.

Now switch legs. Don't be surprised if you have greater difficulty maintaining the Running Pose on the second leg. Most people naturally start out by supporting themselves on their dominant leg and find it more difficult to balance on the other leg. This asymmetry is absolutely normal and will be smoothed out during the process of learning.

Well, there it is. You're in the Running Pose. How does it feel? If you're still wavering back and forth and fighting to hold the pose, relax. Stop wasting that energy. Sink down just a touch further and settle into a compact position. Then try it with your eyes closed. You should be perfectly balanced, perfectly at ease. You may not be ready to run that swift 10K yet, but you're ready to learn how.

Chapter 23

*Motion is created
by the destruction of balance...*
Leonardo da Vinci

LEARNING TO FREE FALL

Now that you mastered the Running Pose and are able to stand in it comfortably balanced and full of potential energy, it's time to destroy that balance for the purpose of moving forward down the road. Because, while mastery of the Pose Method of Running involves many elements, the first hurdle is to overcome our primal fear of falling and turn what we normally fear into an asset that will allow us to run better.

It is our natural inclination to protect the body from falling. What we call "balance" is our ability to stay on our feet and avoid falling to the ground, no matter what we are doing. To learn to run better, we have to learn to do both – fall and avoid hitting the ground.

While this may seem somewhat of a radical concept, remember our previous discussion of Leonardo da Vinci. It was, after all, roughly 500 years ago when he observed that motion is created by the destruction of balance and that free falling animals move fastest.

115

So, now it's time to learn to fall – and to develop a sense of the power that falling creates. When we stand at rest, we are using balance and support to suppress the force of gravity and keep it at bay. The potential to unleash the power of gravity is always present. All we have to do to is to point the body in a given direction, remove our point of support from the ground and see what happens.

A quick demonstration can show you just how much power gravity has. Stand comfortably with your feet about shoulder's width, your knees slightly bent and your weight centered on the balls of your feet with your heels barely in contact with the ground. Then begin leaning to your left side and lift your left foot off the ground, starting a fall to the left (Fig. 23.1). Instead of arresting the fall by thrusting your left leg further out to the left, cross your right leg over in front of the left leg to continue the "fall" to the left. Continue making quick cross steps as you move to the left. Your objective is to let gravity move you in a sideways direction while at the same time avoiding an actual fall by quickly changing your support from one foot to the next.

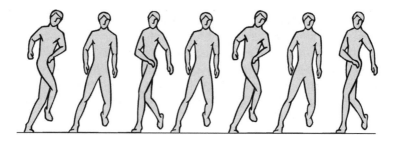

Fig. 23.1. Move with small criss-cross steps leaning the body sideways

When you get the hang of it, you'll realize that you can move pretty quickly without doing any of things you normally associate with "running". First, because you are moving sideways, you have limited the amount of surface area of your foot that comes into contact with the ground. You simply can't land on your heel and continue this sideways movement. By the same token, by moving sideways, your foot is perpendicular to the direction of the fall, not parallel to it, as is usually the case. This lessens amount of time you remain on support on any given foot. By removing the possibility of landing on the heel and rolling all the way through the foot, you get on and off the foot much faster, resulting in a higher cadence.

As you continue making your crisscross steps, you'll also notice that you simply can't straighten your legs or push off your feet and that you have to keep your weight centered on the balls of your feet. In fact, the only thing that both keeps you from falling to the ground and moving faster is the rate at which you change support from one foot to the next.

So now you're moving – quickly – without landing on your heel, without pushing off from your foot and without making any great muscular effort. Gravity is doing all the work and all you're doing is allowing it to happen by falling freely and changing support. Realizing that you can move faster by allowing gravity to do the work than you can by calling into play your own muscular efforts is the key to forming the correct psychological structure for adopting the Pose Method of Running. You will run faster if you free gravity to move your body than you can by the sheer force of your own efforts.

With that in mind, here a few other demonstrations to further drive home the point. You'll need to recruit a partner for these little exercises, which are all very simple, but clearly illustrate the relationship between gravity and forward momentum.

For the first, stand in the running pose and have your partner place on open palm on the center of your chest. Lean slightly forward on the palm until your partner's outstretched hand lightly supports your weight. When your partner pulls the hand away unexpectedly, you automatically start moving forward, without any muscular effort whatsoever. Gravity did all the work, yet you're accelerating rather nicely in the direction you want to go.

So now that you're moving forward, what exactly are your legs supposed to do? If you were to do this without any preliminary explanation, you would put your effort into landing the swing leg on support (Fig. 23.2), while ignoring your support leg. Why? Simply put, because it is our instinct to avoid danger. We are hard-wired to prevent any harm coming to ourselves and fear of falling is ingrained in our psyches. We sense a fall coming and we automatically take preventive action, in this case rushing to put a second leg on the ground while the first one stays put.

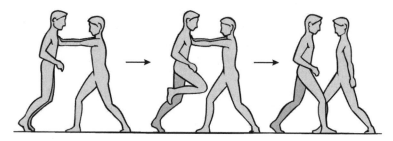

Fig. 23.2. Fall forward
When you are falling, the first instinctive reaction is to bring your foot forward in front of the body to prevent the body from falling

Of course this prevents a fall, but it doesn't keep us moving. In fact, aggressively working your swing leg toward the ground is a braking motion, not a running motion. So to truly learn to free fall and use the Pose Method of Running, you're going to have to overcome deep-seated instincts and let your body fall.

Since we have already concluded that there is a direct correlation between the degree of freedom of running (that is of speed, economy, and efficiency) and the degree of freedom of free falling, we now have to consciously shift our efforts from actively landing on support to actively removing the support leg from the ground. Gravity will do the work to insure that the swing leg makes it back to the ground; it's our job to lift the support foot off the ground as rapidly and efficiently as possible.

Now let's go back and repeat the exercise where your partner supports you with an open palm, then lets you fall (Fig. 23.3). This time, focus your thoughts not on putting your swing leg down, but on lifting your support leg up. This frees gravity to pull you forward while the swing leg gently touches down, pulled there by gravity, without any muscular intervention. Now you're running!

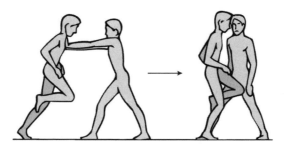

Fig. 23.3. Fall forward and pull the support foot from the ground instead of putting the airborne leg on the ground, in order to unleash the gravity force

Immediately, you'll find yourself accelerating down the trail, free and easy. Now, instead of pounding the pavement, you have combined reduced muscular effort and a very soft landing on the ground the result being a very relaxed running style.

After this exercise, while you're still grasping the freedom of running with gravity, have your partner move to your side and hold his fingertips lightly on your back as you run (Fig. 23.4). His job is not to help you or push you, just touch your back. Try it for 10 or 15 steps and then ask yourself a few questions. What did you feel? Was it easier to run? Why?

While your partner offered no physical assistance, he (or she) made you aware

Fig. 23.4. Running with your partner's hand on your back

of your posture. By subconsciously trying to move away from your partner's hand, you automatically adjusted your posture to a more inclined, sloping, forward-falling position. In other words, you were letting gravity do the job of acceleration. All you had to do was change support to keep up.

Next, if you're still having a problem "getting it", have your partner backpedal while still holding his hand lightly in front of your chest (Fig. 23.5). "Chase" his hand with your chest, leaning forward to stay in contact as much as possible. This should reinforce the feeling of constantly falling forward as you shift support from one foot to the next. You're not using longer strides to keep up; you're just falling forward.

Fig. 23.5. Running with your partner's hand on your chest

For a visual image of the need to free-fall, picture an unicyclist. To move forward, the unicyclist simply leans forward and then pedals fast enough to stay upright. If the unicyclist falls faster than he pedals, the result is a face-plant. The speed of pedaling must match the speed of the fall, so that the unicyclist keeps moving.

The exact same principles are at work in the Pose Method of Running. The greater your forward lean, the faster you must change support in order to stay upright. Greater lean plus faster change of support equals faster running...without greater muscular effort.

While these exercises and visualizations might seem overly simplistic, they really are the key to your psychological acceptance of what it means to fall freely, which is the underlying principle of the Pose Method of Running.

Chapter 24

Practice is the best of all instructors.
Publilius Syrus

DEVELOPING SENSATIONS
OF FREE FALLING

At this point, you should have the first clues of what the Pose Method of Running feels like. The simple partner drills are intended to be the first breakthrough, to demonstrate for the first time that there is a difference between pounding the pavement and flowing down the road under the force of gravity.

But this doesn't mean that you're ready to start piling on the miles quite just yet. With just a taste of the feeling, it would be quite easy for you to revert to your old running style, while convincing yourself that you had changed everything. As the old saying goes, " a little knowledge is a dangerous thing."

The next step is to deeply ingrain the sensations of running with gravity instead of against it. The key to this is to emphasize all of your muscular efforts in removing your support foot from the ground. While this sounds very simple, you would be very surprised how much effort you normally invest in doing things like

121

swinging your leg forward or even putting your foot back down on the ground.

While it is obvious that your foot eventually will make it to the ground (where else can it go, really?) most of us unconsciously push it downward, with surprising force. Not only does this waste energy, it can also lead to injury as the combined effects of gravity and our downward force cause our feet and legs to jar into the ground over and over again.

So it's vital that we truly perfect the art of running with precision and touch. While the objective is to remove the foot from the ground perfectly, this can only be done if it was placed on the ground properly in the first place. If you land on

Fig. 24.1. Landing on toes strains your ankle and forces you to push off

the toes, you're going to "push off" (Fig. 24.1). If you land on your heels, you're going to "roll through" your foot (Fig. 24.2). To take off from the balls of the feet, you have to land there – perfectly – every time.

Fig. 24.2.a Landing on the heel makes you roll through the foot and increase your time on the support

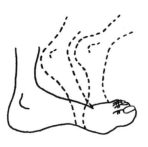

Fig. 24.2.b Foot rolling off of support

Thus, the following exercises are really "baby steps," designed to heighten your sensation of free falling, one drill at a time. Not only should you take the time to perfect these drills before you start serious run training, but you should return to them from time to time over the course of your lifetime of running. Don't let the apparent simplicity of these drills fool you; you may find it completely vexing to do something as easy as letting your foot drop to the ground without forcing it down. Take your time and make sure you "get it" before you move from one drill to the next.

The Pony

Stand in the Running Pose, both knees slightly bent, the ankle of the non-support foot slightly elevated (Fig. 24.3). Simultaneously lift the ankle of the support foot while allowing your body weight to shift to the opposite leg, which is relaxed and falling. Sounds simple, doesn't it. It is, but you have to focus on the following sensations in order to it properly:

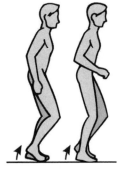

1) Initiate every movement by lifting the support leg, not by pushing down on the non-support leg;

2) Lift the support ankle vertically, with neither forward or backward direction;

3) Shift your weight without inducing any muscular tension;

Fig. 24.3 Pony

4) Allow the non-support leg to fall.

That's a lot to think about for a drill that involves no forward motion, isn't it. At first, perform the pony one change of support at a time, concentrating on staying relaxed and tension free. Then proceed to eliminate the pause between support changes, until you can effortlessly change support from one foot to the next with minimal muscular effort.

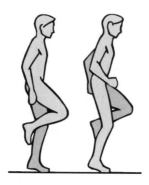

Fig. 24.4 Changing support while moving forward

Changing Support Forward

This drill basically puts the pony in motion. As always you start in the Running Pose (Fig. 24.4). Lean slightly forward and simultaneously pull your support foot straight up and allow the non-support foot to fall to the ground under the center of your body, which, due to your forward lean, will place it slightly ahead of the support foot. Pause to make sure that the weight transfer took place without effort and that you <u>allowed</u> the foot to fall. You want to make sure you're not forcing it down.

As with the pony, you can then begin to eliminate the pause between weight transfers. You're not running, you're just inching your way up the road, maintaining the Running Pose, a relaxed forward lean, easily removing the support foot from the ground and expending minimal muscular effort. As you become confident, you can make slight hops on your support leg, so that you can get the sensation of actively removing your foot from support.

Foot Tapping

This drill emphasizes vertical leg action (Fig. 24.5). Many people think of "running" as an action that begins with lifting the knees and then driving forward. In fact, that's the last thing you want to do. Lifting the knees put tension on the quadriceps and takes you completely out of the Running Pose. Instead, you want to lift the ankle, vertically, so that the ankle, hip, shoulder and head remain in a straight line. So instead of lifting the knee, you want to lift the ankle. This prevents your

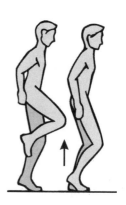

Fig. 24.5. Foot tapping

foot from getting out in front of the body and allows the leg to bend quickly with minimal muscular force. (Do you see a trend here? Everything is done to minimize extraneous muscular effort.)

Start, as usual, in the Running Pose, holding the non-support ankle with the ankle slightly elevated. Let the non-support leg drop to the ground by simply relaxing all your leg muscles, while remaining standing in place with your weight on the support leg. Allow your non-support leg to tap the ground, with the hamstring "firing" to remove it from the ground as soon as it hits. As you get the feel of it, increase the range of motion, lifting your ankle higher and higher with each repetition. While keeping your quadriceps completely relaxed, you should be able to lift your heel all the way to your pelvis with minimal effort. As you increase the range of motion, resist the temptation to increase your tempo, by forcing your foot back down. If you don't stay focused, you could soon find yourself virtually slamming your foot back to the ground.

Concentrate on the following:

1) Rapid firing of the hamstring. If you are working with a partner, have him or her gently tap your hamstring every time your foot touches down. This will cue you to fire your hamstring and initiate early muscular contraction.

2) Keep your entire musculature relaxed after the initial firing of the hamstring. If you're successful at this, your leg will decelerate as it is going up, then accelerate as it drops back down. Both the slowing down and the speeding up will be due to gravity, <u>not muscular effort</u>. Remember – don't continue lifting your leg. Just fire the hamstring once and then let gravity take over.

Hopping

With this drill, the exercises become a little dynamic and demanding (Fig. 24.6). You may think of hopping as child's play, but it's actually a very advanced pliometric drill that develops muscular power, agility, muscular relaxation and the neuro-

125

muscular programming that prompts rapid vertical removal of the foot from the ground once initial contact is made.

Please note that hopping is a drill where you can hurt yourself if you don't do it properly. You're not trying to bound all over the place; your objective is to stay in the Running Pose while your remove your support leg from the ground and then allow it to return to the ground, completely relaxed, through the force of gravity.

Fig. 24.6.
Hopping

You should first do your hops barefoot, on a forgiving surface such as grass, sand, mats or synthetic composition surfaces like running tracks. To start, stand in the Running Pose. With the non-support ankle slightly elevated, lift your support foot vertically from the ground through a rapid firing of the hamstring. Allow it to return return to the ground, completely relaxed.

Keep your focus on the following:

1) As with the tapping drills, all your muscles should be completely relaxed after the initial firing of the hamstrings. Judge the tension (or lack of it) in your quadriceps and the springiness in your calves to make sure you are staying relaxed.

2) Don't push with the calf; just lift your ankle rapidly with each hop. Make sure your ankle is relaxed between each hop.

3) If you have trouble maintaining balance, you can start out by having the toes of your non-support foot touch the ground.

Start out your hopping drills by staying in place, hopping several times on one leg, then switching to the other. Work up to the point where your heel actually touches your buttocks – as long as you maintain complete quadriceps relaxation. Please note that this is an exaggerated range of motion whose purpose is to establish a new motor pattern. While you're actually running, you won't attempt to lift your ankle that high.

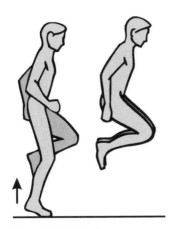

Fig. 24.7. High hopping

After you're comfortable hopping in place, you can hop in a forward direction (Fig. 24.7). Remember that forward hopping is not the result of pushing off from you toes or with the calf. To hop forward, simply lean forward and continue landing with your foot directly under your body.

Forward hops combine two elements of free falling in one drill. In the first place, you're experiencing the free falling of your foot as it returns to the ground in a relaxed state after the hamstring has fired. Secondly, you feel the weight of your body propelled forward by gravity as you lean forward. These are really very complex sensations, and it will require your full attention to avoid doing unnecessary work. As you lean forward. you will be tempted both to push off with your foot and to slam it back down to prevent a fall. Make sure you're completely comfortable with the prior drills before attempting hopping drills and stop if you find you are not relaxed while performing the exercise.

Front Lunges

While you may be familiar with lunges from visits to health clubs, the front lunges you perform here are slightly different and you must perform them correctly to aid your hamstring development and continue the process of developing the sensations of free falling. The body position is familiar with the weight of the body on the forward leg and the rear leg only used for balance and stability

127

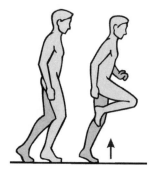

Fig. 24.8. Front lunge

(Fig. 24.8). The objective again is to pull the front leg from support using only the hamstring with minimal assist from any other muscles or muscles groups. The lunge position truly isolates the hamstring and forces you to work with it and no other muscles.

Start out by doing the exercise in place until you feel that you are stable and working only with the hamstring. Then allow some forward movement, created not by pushing off from the ground, but only by leaning forward (Fig. 24.9). Then, straighten up a little more and approximate one-

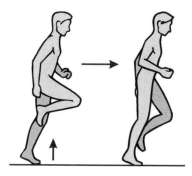

Fig. 24.9. Forward front lunge

legged running, still using only your hamstring for lift and only a forward lean for movement, while dragging your rear leg behind you for balance. This progression is key in creating the simple biomechanical framework of the Pose Method: the hamstring does the work and gravity pulls you forward.

Skipping

As with hopping, you may consider skipping to be another childhood romp. And that's the beauty of childhood...a lot of the things you did for fun were actually very good exercise. Start in the elastic position on two legs and begin with easy jumps where one leg is simultaneously pulled up directly under the pelvis (Fig. 24.10). As with normal skipping, land on two legs. As with the other exercises, proceed from skipping in place to moving forward, then alternate the feet that are pulled up and finally vary your

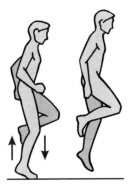

tempo…moderate, quick, moderate, quick and so on.

Fig. 24.10. Skipping

Chapter 25

*A journey of a thousand miles
must begin with a single step.*
Lo-Tzu

GOING FOR A RUN

Wow! Here you are roughly halfway through a book on running and you've yet to do what you love most: just go out for a run. If you've been even remotely diligent about proceeding through all the steps of learning the Pose Method, you've just got to be burning to put on your favorite running kit, lace up the shoes and head out the door for a good old fashioned run.

To this point, you've read arguments for the Pose Method, mulled over concepts of the Pose Method, put yourself through drills to experience the sensations of the Pose Method...I wouldn't blame you if you never wanted to hear the words "Pose Method" ever again.

But there's still the question of getting out the door and running with the new technique that you've only just tasted in your drills. Later in the book we'll discuss how fear is a reflection of personal uncertainty, but right now it's safe to say that you're probably a little uncertain and a little scared to 'just go for a run' using the Pose Method technique.

Before you ever heard of the Pose Method, your thoughts, both before and during a run, no doubt centered on what route you would run, how far and how fast you would go, not to mention the many extraneous thoughts of personal responsibilities and activities that seem to creep into your mind during the relatively idle hours you spend on the roads and trails. But it's probably safe to say that you spent relatively little time thinking about *how* you would run. The act of running itself was just something you did reflexively, not something you agonized over.

But now, quite unexpectedly, you have to think about how you're going to actually commit the act of running. You might even say to yourself, "I'll just run my 'natural' style while I keep learning the Pose Method." Or you might be committed to run Pose style, but remain very uncertain about how far you should go, how fast, whether you should try any hills and, worst of all, if the running you're doing is really the Pose Method.

It's a lot to think about, and chances are you're not even comfortable thinking about running that much. Relax. Yes, it's a lot to think about, but the challenge of turning theory into practice in anything is always a big hurdle. You're going to get through this, and once you do, you're never going to look back.

Right now, you're thinking about speed, distance, hills/no hills and myriad other things. What you should be thinking about is changing support from one foot to the next. Yes, as that most trite of folk sayings insists, the longest journey begins with but a single step, and in this case the journey is the future of your running lifetime and that first step should be as perfect as possible. Get the first one right and all the others that follow stand an excellent chance of being just as good.

And that's really the sum and point of all your Pose Method training, to take perfect steps. It does not matter how far you intend to run or how fast, as long as you make perfect steps, you will run well. Of course that's a lot of pressure to put on a first step. One of America's most quotable athletes, Yogi Berra, once said "How can you think and hit at the same time?"

Now you're faced with the prospect of thinking and running at the same time, which means it's time to go back to basics. You're out the door, dressed for a run, ready to take that perfect first step. First, run through your checklist. Are you relaxed and balanced? Standing in the running pose, with knees slightly bent? Breathing easily? That's good, but before you take off, stand up straight for a minute and mentally rehearse what you expect to happen.

First, you're going to remove one of your feet from support, initiate a forward fall, lift your trunk imperceptibly and ...what?...run! Just as you did in your drills, you're going to pull your support foot away from the ground, directly under your body, and begin moving under the force of gravity. In the very next instant, you're going to continue the fall by removing the other foot from the ground as quickly as possible. And then you're going to do it over and over again.

Yes, it is as simple as that. But being simple doesn't mean being easy, because what you have to accomplish is happening not over the long period of time implied by the term *distance running,* but over the instant of a single step, a relative blink of the eye. A long run is nothing more than a collection of perfect steps, all of which take place in the shortest time frame.

How short? For the record, the world's best runners remain in contact for roughly one tenth of a second, slower runners perhaps twice that long. That's the amount of time per stride (or step) that you spend in the running pose, between one and two tenths of a second. And that's where everything has to be perfect. Every time one of your feet comes in contact with the ground, you should still be relaxed, resilient, knees slightly bent, foot directly at the bottom of the line that runs straight down from your head through your hips and feet.

So now you've taken that first step and you're off and running, all the while processing information, asking yourself questions. Does it feel right? Am I falling forward? Am I pulling up with the hamstring? Have I stayed in the Running Pose and in my frame?

It's one thing to think about things in the abstract, quite another to think about them while you're actually in action. If you worry too much about how you're running, you can actually fall victim to that old plague "paralysis by analysis." So to simplify the thought process while running, to stay smooth and focused, concentrate your thoughts on the keep points of the Pose Method of Running.

The main elements to keep in mind are the Pose, the Fall and the Pull. You maintain the Running Pose, you fall forward and you pull up with the hamstring. As you run, you can quickly run through that checklist over and over again, until it becomes a sort of mantra for your run.

1) Check the pose: Am I relaxed and balanced? Am I landing lightly on the ball of my foot, with my foot directly underneath my body? Are my knees still bent?
2) Check the fall: Do I have any muscular tension? Am I braking myself with any body part? Am I leaning with my whole body?
3) Check the foot pull: Am I pulling my foot...and not my leg? Am I pulling the instant my foot touches the ground? Am I pulling straight up?

As you settle into the run, this mantra or formula for your run can be shortened into a rhythm. Pose-fall-pull, Pose-fall-pull. Run through this formula as you run down the road and you find yourself very centered on the act of running and not on the *results* of running. Instead of thinking about how far or how fast you are running or how tired you may be getting, you've dialed yourself into the essentials of the run.

Once you settle into the rhythm, you can even control the tempo of your run by increasing the speed of the mantra. Go from pose—fall—pull to pose-fall-pull to posefallpull and not only will you feel your speed increasing, but you'll feel your body lean further forward and your feet lift more quickly from the ground. You'll also hear the change in the sound your feet make as they tap the ground. Everything gets lighter, faster, more focused and, yes, more fun. Try variations on the rhythm mantra until you find one that works for you. Count strides 1-2-3-4, 1-2-3-4 or merely repeat up-up-up-up in time with every foot strike. As you find your stride and your rhythm, it becomes an intellectual game to see how long you can hold your form together as you blast down the road faster and faster.

From a technical standpoint, it is actually easier to run fast than it is to run slowly in the Pose Method. Where before you might have run like a wheezing pick-up truck, with the Pose Method you now have the technology of a race car built into your body, and everybody knows that race cars love to move fast. At slow speeds, you <u>are</u> staying too long on support, you <u>are</u> standing up too straight, you <u>are</u> landing with too much of a thud, but as you accelerate, everything smoothes out. Your running machine begins firing on all cylinders.

Okay, so maybe it's a bit of a stretch to think you'll go gunning down the road like a finely tuned Ferrari on your first real Pose Method run, but the point is that you can't be afraid to use your new style. If you head out the door full of trepidation, scared of your own shadow, and try to run really, really slow, just to make sure that you're doing it right, you probably won't be doing it right at all.

Embrace your new running technique. Take it out for a spin. See how it feels. It *is* fun to run, and the better you run, the more fun it is. The first few times, don't pay any attention to how far or fast you go and don't be afraid to stop if at any time you feel like you're doing something wrong.

In fact, it's a good idea to stop frequently, review the feelings you've been having and make sure they're consistent with what you know you should be doing in the Pose Method. Think about your run, decide what corrections need to be made and then start over again. This way, you're always fresh when you run and you don't let improper technique become a part of your style.

Tune in to your body when you run. Strive for lightness, quickness, suppleness. Listen to the sound of your feet tapping and consciously make the sound grow more faint. Feel for the rapid contraction of the hamstring when your foot touches the ground. Control your breathing, keep your face impassive, make no unnecessary motions. Conserve your energy. And above all, enjoy running.

You have made the transition from thought to action. You are now a Pose Method runner. With that thought in mind, it is now time to build up the capacity of your body and your mind to become the best runner you can possibly be.

Section V

BUILDING A RUNNER'S BODY...AND MIND

Chapter 26

*A chain is no stronger
than its weakest link.*
Proverb

STRENGTH CONDITIONING FOR RUNNING

At the dawn of America's running boom in the 70s, virtually no one in the self-coached running community paid attention to strength development as it applied to running. In fact, it could be said that quite the opposite was true. To the newly ordained devotees, running was all about escaping the confines of sweaty gyms and reveling in the freedom of the great outdoors. For many, running was a positive addiction, a chance to spiritually invigorate the body and escape the normal strictures of daily life.

Conversely, the image of strength development was seen to be entirely separate from running. Weight lifters and body builders were viewed as muscle bound denizens of dank gyms, where a word-of-mouth subculture was already trading in anabolic steroids and other strength products. The two worlds could not have been further apart.

To get better at running, the theory went, all you had to do was run more...and more...and more. The school of LSD (Long Slow Distance) was given credence by the remarkable success of mega-mileage runners like Frank Shorter, Bill Rodgers and Alberto Salazar. Good runners were skinny, if not downright emaciated; weight lifters were huge, immobile chunks of humanity.

While most runners of the era were self-trained, this disdain extended to the coaches of the time. They too were on the "longer is better" bandwagon and simply didn't consider strength development an essential element in the training regime. Instead of thinking about the overall development of the human organism, coaches focused on the cardiovascular and respiratory systems as the key to enhanced performance. High volumes of training, went the theory, would improve these systems and result in ever-faster marathon performances.

However, as we have previously discussed, the results of this training scenario were not faster times, but a gradual deterioration of America's status in the running world and a generation of broken down runners. In retrospect, it was always a formula for disaster: combine high mileage with poor technique and the absence of strength training and the result will be injured runners.

By the end of the 70s, it was becoming clear to the more enlightened coaches that LSD by itself was not the program for success. As injuries mounted up in both the "professional" and amateur ranks and America ceded its position of temporary dominance in the marathon, it was obvious that a new approach was necessary.

However, the fact that a few coaches here and there began to rethink the strength training issue did not have an immediate effect. Since most amateur runners were self-trained, there was quite a defection in the ranks of sport runners, who simply concluded that running was too rough on the body to continue as a lifetime sport. Many found more attractive alternatives in cycling and swimming and in fact turned to triathlon as a way to run less but still stay in shape.

So while the masses of fun runners looked for new outlets for their training enthusiasms, serious coaches were trying out new programs to re-balance the body for the rigors of running. Most of this experimentation took place in isolation and there was no general consensus on how to best strengthen the body to run.

One beacon of clarity citing the need to develop strength as essential came in 1978 from the Runner's Handbook, in which authors Bob Glover and Jack Shepherd specifically named "weak feet" and "weak anti-gravity muscles" as two of the 10 principle causes of injury-causing trauma in running. Noting that, "Track coaches are now recommending weight programs for their men and women runners," the two were outspoken proponents of strength training (1).

However, while their insight never truly penetrated the thinking of mainstream runners, thinking has now come full circle. The efforts of leading scientists and coaches have now been acknowledged and the value of strength conditioning for achieving endurance running results has been undeniably proven.

But if the Pose Method of Running is so simple, relying specifically on gravity for momentum and the rapid release of the foot from the ground, you may wonder why strength training is so vital. How, in fact, can strength development contribute to running improvement?

Forgive, for a moment, one of the most overused clichés in the English language, but it really is true that a chain is only as strong as its weakest link. The human body is not a collection of independently operating muscle groups, but instead is an integrated system of those muscle groups. When your objective is to propel the body forward through space and time, every fiber of your being has a role to play and must be prepared to contribute to the overall successful functioning of the integrated system. A breakdown in just one area will lead to reduced performance and ultimately the breakdown of the entire system.

In the Pose Method of Running, the movements are very simple and repetitive, but there is a substantial requirement of strength not only to perform those movements, but also to not perform extraneous movements that will drain energy and detract from the overall performance.

For a very visual analogy, think of an old style locomotive train. The actual transfer of energy from the engine to the wheels is accomplished by a simple mechanical system that pushes a rod down on the drive wheels – over and over again. In other words, simple, repetitive movements are used to drive mammoth amounts of steel and cargo and passengers across thousands of miles and over the highest mountains. The movements are simple and the range of motion is completely contained and never varies; yet the requirements for strength are tremendous. In order for the integrated system to continue to function, every element in the system must be designed for maximum power.

In the Pose Method of Running, the primary movement – releasing the foot from the ground – is very simple, yet the body must be conditioned and disciplined so that there is no wild swinging of arms, no overstriding and no excessive vertical oscillation. To continue to stay within the running frame without deviation for mile after mile after mile requires not only mental focus but also a body that is prepared to deliver what the mind demands of it.

While there is a substantial need for strength to maintain the discipline required to operate within the running frame, strength also contributes to another vital component of success – quickness. Your first thought may be to say that as a long distance runner, you don't need quickness. You may in fact think of quickness as an attribute of cornerbacks in football or point guards in basketball…and of course, track's 100-meter runners.

But what role does quickness play in distance running? Actually, it is absolutely vital. The two primary elements of the speed you are able to maintain as you run are: 1) the amount of time it takes you to release your foot from support and 2) your overall running cadence. Both of these elements require both muscular elasticity and the strength to maintain it over time. Common sense tells you that the stronger you are, the longer you will be able to maintain the quick rhythm of any repetitive motion, particularly one that supports your entire body weight.

Moreover, when you combine the requirements of staying within the running frame, performing repetitive movements quickly and having the endurance to do this over an extended period of time, a larger picture emerges. What at first seems like the science of mechanical requirements morphs into something much more subtle, more art than science.

Just as the repetitive movements that comprise ballet, figure skating or springboard diving are perceived as artistic, the overall perfection a skilled runner brings to his sport transcends mere function and evolves into something truly beautiful. And it is not a case of "legs running" but instead an overall performance of an integrated system, the human body, mastering a specific technique and performing it flawlessly.

At this level, where performance becomes art, we leave the realm of mere numbers and distances and focus instead on the total picture of a perfectly functioning human being flowing through time and space.

Fig. 26.1. Cheetah's run

A quick mental image may help here. Think of slow motion nature footage you have seen of cheetahs (Fig. 26.1) or other swift animals running in "chase" mode. The absolute perfection and beauty of their movements is evident even to the most unschooled eyes. No matter the terrain, these animals move with alarming speed and complete focus. When you watch them, you are struck not only by their prowess, but also by their suppleness. Even as you comprehend their enormous strength, what you see are very loose and flexible muscles flowing to and fro as they move.

What you want to do is become the cheetah. Substitute yourself into the mental image and watch yourself run over the same terrain. Do you flow smoothly, seemingly suspended above the ground, or do you bog down and eventually give up, unable to continue the chase?

The importance of strength training for running is to give you the physical capacity to flow like nature's best runners. Once you have mastered the basic elements of the Pose Method of Running, you must *become* a runner, in the Zen sense of the word. You must develop the quickness, the strength and the vision to run without becoming a slave either to the dictates of the stopwatch or to the environment in which you are running.

From a practical standpoint, this requires very specific preparation that will take the disparate muscle systems of your body and fuse them into a single system ready to run. A poorly prepared body, without sufficient strength development, will prematurely display all the trademarks of poor running technique: elongated stride, clumsy movement, general slowness and facial evidence of psychological and emotional discomfort. Conversely, the properly prepared runner will move with a quick, compact stride and will have a serene, focused countenance.

The following types of exercises fulfill the requirements for basic strength conditioning for runners:
      A) Muscular elasticity development (Chapter 27)
      B) Hip muscles conditioning (Chapter 28)
      C) Hamstrings conditioning (Chapter 29)

For those new to strength conditioning, the process of undertaking an entirely new exercise regime may seem daunting. Chapter 30 explains the process by which this vital strength training can be successfully integrated.

The ability to deal with varying terrain doesn't just happen because of your ability to generate the appropriate mental imagery. You must experience and prepare for the real life challenges presented by running in different environments. Specific exercises and techniques for all the following situations will be detailed in later chapters:

A) Sand running (Chapter 31)
B) Running uphill and downhill (Chapter 32)
C) Trail running (Chapter 33)
D) Barefoot running (Chapter 34)

This list isn't meant to exclude any other exercises you may want to incorporate into your overall routine, but these exercises are necessary to optimize your running potential. Remember, there are no bad exercises, per se, but there may be poorly performed or poorly implemented exercises that will not contribute to your overall development.

1. Glover, B. and Shepherd, J., 1978, Runner's Handbook, p. 121.

Chapter 27

DEVELOPING MUSCULAR ELASTICITY

While the development of muscular elasticity is crucial in improving your overall running performance, your progress is somewhat difficult to quantify. As your work through your program, the evidence may first come in terms of the ease with which you achieve quicker stride rates, which in turn signifies greater mechanical efficiency.

The various jumping exercises that promote elasticity do not require a lot of time to perform, but you must be careful to perform them correctly and not overdo it at first. For such seemingly easy exercises, they hold the potential for both injury and soreness. Proceed cautiously and master the jumps before you increase the number of repetitions and/or sets.

The most important aspect of these jumping exercises is that your objective is NOT to push off from the ground, but instead to pull your feet from the ground using your hamstrings. No doubt your current visual imagery of jumping would be the centers jumping at the opening tip-off of a basketball game. You know the image: the centers hunker down, knees bent, and then explode toward the sky as the referee throws the ball into the air, pushing off for all they are worth. Forget that image.

In these exercises, the objective is to center the explosion in the hamstrings, pulling your feet rapidly from the ground. There is but a single pull, performed as rapidly as possible, and then the hamstring immediately relaxes. At the same time, you must be alert to keep your legs bent at all times. The knees should never be straightened.

The first sets of jumps are fixed-position jumps, performed standing in one place (Figs. 27.1-27.14). These should be perfected before you try directional jumps.

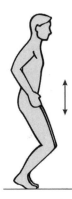

Fig. 27.1. Bouncing up-down in S(spring)-like position on two legs

Fig. 27.2. Jumps on two legs in S(spring)-like position on two legs with toes pulled up

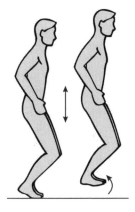

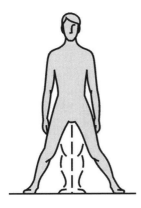

*Fig. 27.3. Jumps
with feet together
and apart*

*Fig. 27.4. Jumps
upward with feet
together and apart*

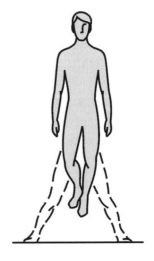

Fig. 27.5. Jumps forward from the S(spring)-like position

Fig. 27.6. Jumps from a front lunge switching legs

*Fig. 27.7. Jumps
on two legs turning
toes in and out*

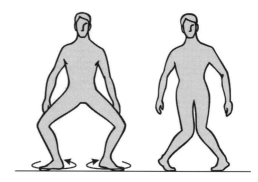

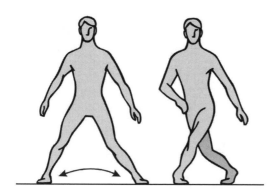

*Fig. 27.8. Jumps
with legs crossing
in front*

Fig. 27.9. Jumps twisting hips while holding legs together

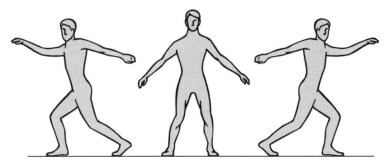

Fig. 27.10. Jumps turning feet from side to side

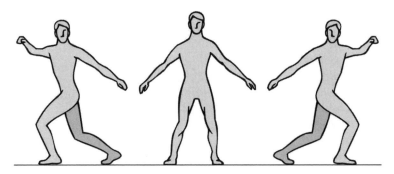

Fig. 27.11. Jumps twisting hips and landing in front lunge

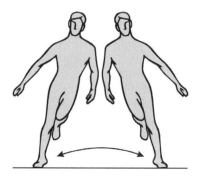

Fig. 27.12. Jumps shifting the body weight from one leg to the other ("ice skating")

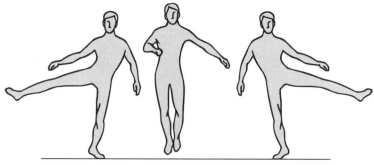

Fig. 27.13. Jumps shifting body weight from one leg to the other by swinging legs side to side("side pendulum")

Fig. 27.14. Jumps shifting body weight from one leg to the other by swinging legs back and forth ("forward pendulum")

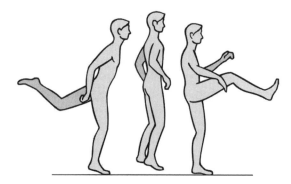

In performing the directional jumps (Figs. 27.15-27.29), you will move your body forward, backward or sideways, jumping with one or both legs. You must resist the temptation to achieve the directional movement by pushing with your legs. Instead, use body lean to guide your direction, just as you do when you run in the Pose Method. Don't push, just lean.

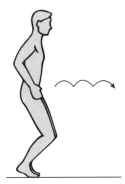

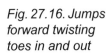

Fig. 27.15.
Hops forward
on two legs

Fig. 27.16. Jumps
forward twisting
toes in and out

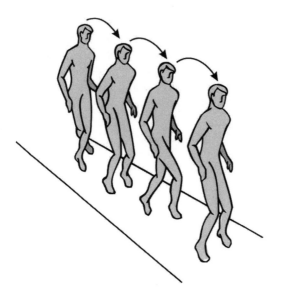

Fig. 27.17.
Jumps forward
crossing legs

Fig. 27.18.
Jumps forward
turning feet left
and right

154

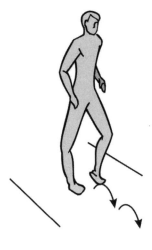

Fig. 27.19.
Jumps forward
on lateral sides
of feet

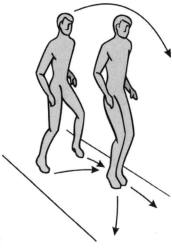

Fig. 27.20. Jumps
forward bringing
feet together and
apart

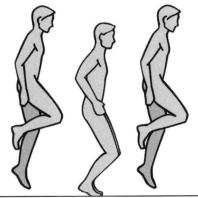

Fig. 27.21. Skips
on one leg

Fig. 27.22. Skips alternating legs

Fig. 27.23. Hops forward on one leg turning the foot in and out

Fig. 27.24. Hops forward on one leg holding the other foot aside

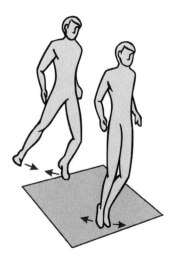

Fig. 27.25.
Hops forward
on one leg

Fig. 27.26. Hops
sideways on one
leg holding the
other foot in front

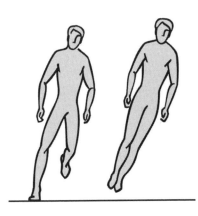

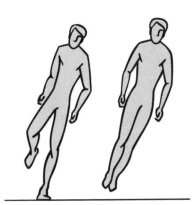

Fig. 27.27. Hops
sideways on one
leg holding the
other foot back

Fig. 27.28. Jumps forward from one leg to the other

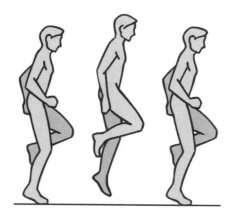

Fig. 27.29. Hops forward alternating the legs

When jumping with weights (bar, dumbbells, heavy belts) (Figs. 27.30-27.40), all movements of your body must be synchronized. Where the initial fixed-position and directional jumps focused primarily on strength development through elasticity, the jumps with weights and stretch cord resistance add in the component of coordinated movement and reinforce the concept of integrated body movement. A runner performing perfectly does not appear to be a collection of disparate parts moving randomly, but instead resembles a beautifully flowing mechanism. When you practice these jumps, be sure that everything moves at once, that you are a machine working in perfect harmony.

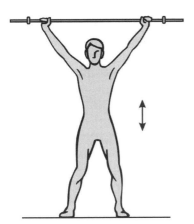

Fig. 27.30. Hops on two legs with the bar above the head

Fig. 27.31. Same as Fig. 27.30, bringing legs together and apart

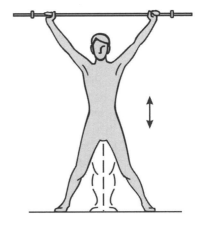

Fig. 27.32. Hops with the bar, legs together and apart

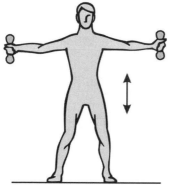

Fig. 27.33. Hops on two legs with dumbbells

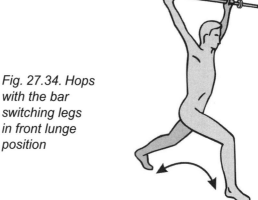

Fig. 27.34. Hops with the bar switching legs in front lunge position

Fig. 27.35.
Jumps with the
bar switching
legs on the box

Fig. 27.36.
Jumps on two
legs with the bar
in one hand

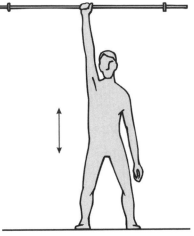

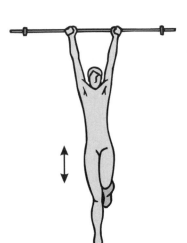

Fig. 27.37.
Jumps on one
leg with the bar
in two hands

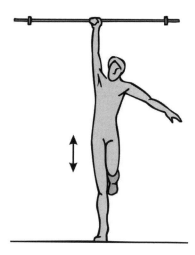

Fig. 27.38. Jumps on one leg with the bar in the same side hand

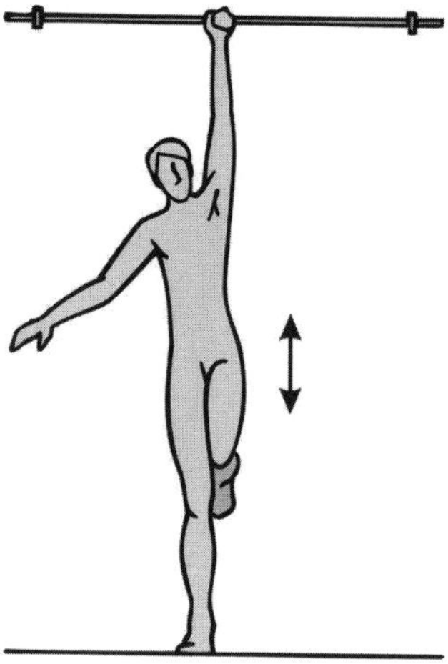

Fig. 27.39. Jumps on one leg with the bar in the opposite side hand

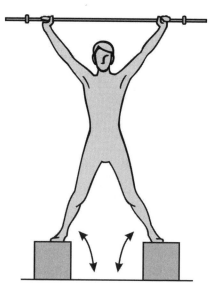

Fig. 27.40. Jumps on two legs to and from boxes with the bar

When moving into the jumps with stretch cord resistance (Figs. 27.41-27.51), be careful once again to hone your movements. Where weights provide passive resistance, the stretch cords actively work against you and can surprise you with their force against your intended movement path. As you get used to the feeling of the stretch cord resistance, you can then focus on the complete integration of your movements. The very resistance of the cords highlights any imperfection of your movements. As your movements improve, the exercises will seem easier and more natural.

Please note that all jumps should be performed on the balls of the feet (the forefoot) just as you do when you run in the Pose Method. These jumps prepare your "movement apparatus" for the real life situations of landing on support, no matter what the terrain underfoot may be.

Fig. 27.41. Jumps on two legs with the rope

Fig. 27.42. Jumps on one leg with the rope

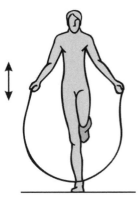

163

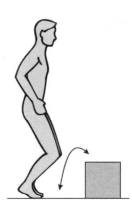

Fig. 27.43. Jumps on two legs to and from the box

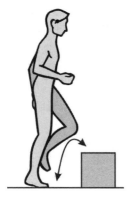

Fig. 27.44. Jumps on one leg to and from the box

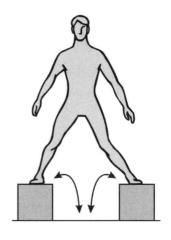

Fig. 27.45. Jumps to and from two boxes

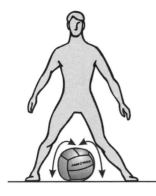

Fig. 27.46. Jumps on two legs to and from the medicine ball

Fig. 27.47. Jumps to and from two medicine balls

Fig. 27.48. Jumps on two legs over medicine balls

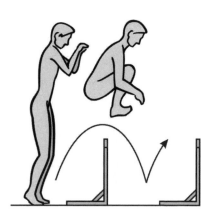

Fig. 27.49. Jumps on two legs over hurdles

Fig. 27.50. Jumps on one leg holding the rear foot on the box

Fig. 27.51. Hops on one leg with the rubber band resistance

Chapter 28

Life grants nothing to us,
mortals, without hard work.
Horace

EXERCISES FOR HIPS

The importance of these exercises lies in the fact that the anatomical and biomechanical position of the hips affects the integrated movement of the whole body. As the bridge between the upper and lower body, the hips play a key role in integrating and coordinating all of the body's movements. The stability and strength of the hips provide the path for mechanical energy flow through the body during support and flight. Further, strong hips provide the foundation for the loads experienced by the lower extremities on support and reduce the impact on the lower back.

Hips exercises in the standing position (Figs. 28.1-28.6) and kneeling position (Figs. 28.7-28.9) promote improved balance skills for running as well as enhance the strength of the muscles in the hips area.

In Standing Position

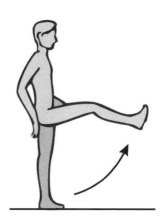

Fig. 28.1. Move the airborne leg up and down in front

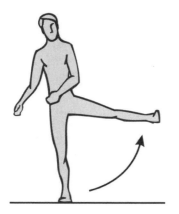

Fig. 28.2. Move the airborne leg up and down sideways

Fig. 28.3. Move the airborne leg backward

Fig. 28.4."Seesaw". Bend the trunk over, touching the ground with your hands and moving the airborne leg backward up

Fig. 28.5. Balance on one leg, bending the trunk over and move the airborne leg up and down sideways

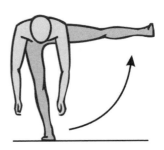

Fig. 28.6. Same as Fig. 28.5, move the airborne leg backward

169

In Kneeling Position

Fig. 28.7. Move the airborne leg up and down in front

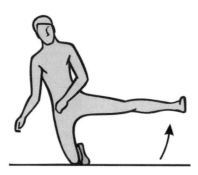

Fig. 28.8. Move the airborne leg up and down sideways

Fig. 28.9. Move the airborne leg backward

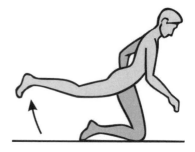

Exercises performed lying down on the ground (Figs. 28.10-28.36) isolate the movement of the hips from the rest of the body, so you can focus your energy on the dynamic movement of this area of the body. These exercises are performed in a variety of positions, including face-up, face-down, face-down with hands in the "push-up" position and with the hands or feet on low objects like small boxes or exercise balls.

Fig. 28.10. Fold the legs over the body and straighten (lift) the body along the wall

Fig. 28.11. Support on the shoulders, feet on the wall, move the hips up and down

Fig. 28.12. Same as Fig.28.11, with one foot on the wall

171

In Lying Down Position

Face Up

Fig. 28.13. Back on the floor, knees bent, with support on the   shoulders and feet, move hips move up and down

Fig. 28.14. Same as Fig.28.13, with one leg on support

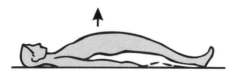

Fig. 28.15. Support on the shoulders and heels, move hips up to form an arch and down

Fig. 28.16. Same as Fig.28.15, with one leg on support and the other in the air

Face Down

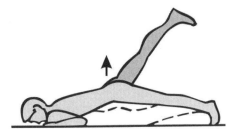

Fig. 28.17. Face down, support on the chest, arms and toes, move hips and the airborne leg up and down

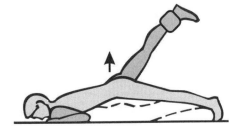

Fig. 28.18. Same as Fig.28.17, add ankle weights

Push Up Position

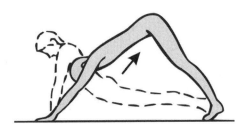

Fig. 28.19. Arms, feet on support – move hips up & down

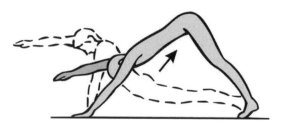

Fig. 28.20. One arm, two feet on support,
move hips up & down

Fig. 28.21. Two arms, one foot on support,
move hips up & down

Fig. 28.22. One arm and the opposite leg on
support, move hips up & down

Fig. 28.23. Same side arm and foot on support,
move hips up & down

Fig. 28.24. Two arms, one foot on
support, the airborne leg held to the
side, move hips up & down

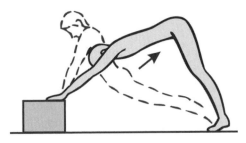

Fig. 28.25. Perform all of the above listed
exercises (Fig.28.19-28.24) with support
on the box

Face Up Position

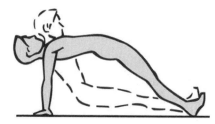

Fig. 28.26. Arms, and feet on support, move hips up & down

Fig. 28.27. One arm, two feet on support, move hips up & down

Fig. 28.28. Two arms, one foot on support, move hips up & down

Fig. 28.29. The opposite arm & foot on support, move hips up & down

Fig. 28.30. The same side arm & foot on support, move hips up & down

Fig. 28.31. Two arms, one foot on support, the airborne leg held to the side, move hips up & down

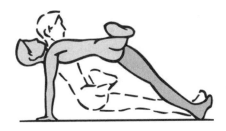

Fig. 28.32. Two arms, one foot on support, twist the airborne leg & hips to the opposite side

Fig. 28.33. Perform all of the above listed exercises (Fig.28.25-28.32) with arms on the box

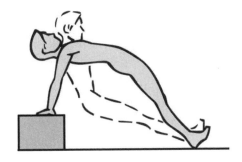

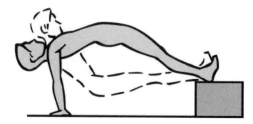

Fig. 28.34. Perform all of the above listed exercises (Fig.28.25-28.32) with feet on the box

Fig. 28.35. Perform all of the above listed exercises (Fig. 28.25-28.32) with arms and feet on two boxes

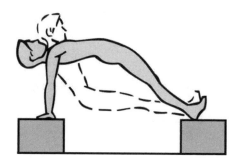

Collectively, these exercises greatly improve your awareness of the role your hips play in overall movement. As the connection to the rest of the body is emphasized or de-emphasized as you move through the exercises, you develop a much higher awareness of the connectivity of your hips to all of your movement. Thus, it becomes much more apparent how vital they are to the integrated movement of your entire body.

Building on that awareness, the sideways exercises (Figs. 28.36-28.40) reintroduce balance as a critical element, while building strength and once again enhancing integration.

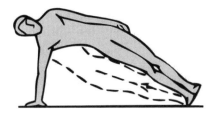

Fig. 28.36. One arm, two feet on support, move hips up & down

Fig. 28.37. One arm, one foot on support, the other one held airborne, move hips up & down

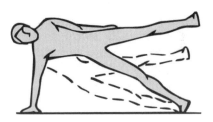

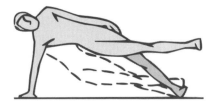

Fig. 28.38. One arm, one foot on support, the other one held airborne, move hips up & down

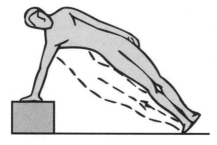

Fig. 28.39. Perform all of the above listed exercises (Fig.28.36-28.38) with one arm support on the box

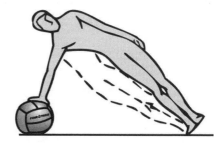

Fig. 28.40. Perform all of the above listed exercises (Fig.28.36-28.38) with one arm support on the medicine ball

Exercises performed with a partner (Figs. 28.41-28.69) add the element of instability, forcing the hips to make micro-adjustments to maintain perfect movement. It is simply impossible for a partner to be absolutely stable as he supports you throughout these exercises. Therefore your hips are forced to develop the strength to adjust for unstable conditions, just as they would during a "real-world" run. When your partner provides the resistance to your movements, he has the ability to feel your efforts and make adjustments in that resistance exactly as required. Whereas weights and stretch-cords are inanimate and unthinking, a partner can respond to your efforts and help guide you with the correct amount of resistance relative to direction, speed and time.

Face Up Position with Partner

Fig. 28.41. Support on two arms, with the partner holding the feet, move hips up & down

Fig. 28.42. Support on one arm, with the partner holding the opposite foot, move hips up & down

Fig. 28.43. Same as Fig.28.42, only the partner is holding the same side foot

Fig. 28.44. Arms on support, with the partner holding one foot, and keeping the airborne leg to the side, move hips up & down

181

Face Down Position with Partner

Fig. 28.45. Support on the arms, with the partner holding the feet, move hips up & down

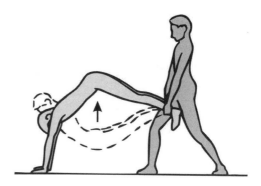

Fig. 28.46. Support on one arm, with the partner holding the opposite foot, move hips up & down

Fig. 28.47. Support on one arm, with the partner holding the same side foot, move hips up & down

With Partner's resistence, Face Up

Fig. 28.48. Support on arms & feet, with the partner's resistance, move hips up & down

Fig. 28.49. Support on one arm & two feet, move hips up & down

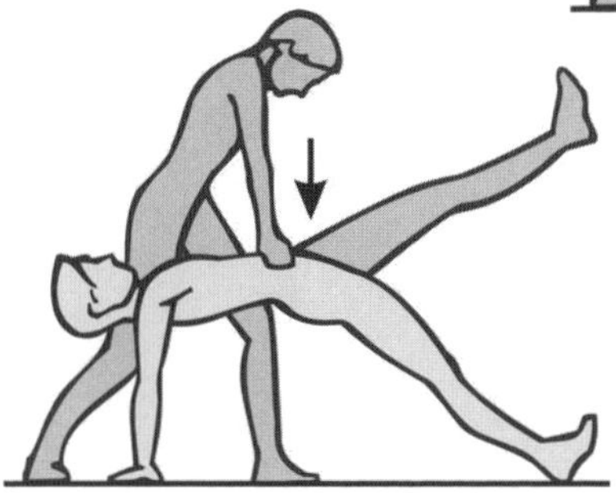

Fig. 28.50. Same as Fig.28.48, holding one leg in the air

Fig. 28.51. Same as Fig.28.49, holding the same side leg in the air

Fig. 28.52. Same as Fig. 28.49, holding the opposite leg in the air

Fig. 28.53. Same as Fig.28.50, holding one leg to the side

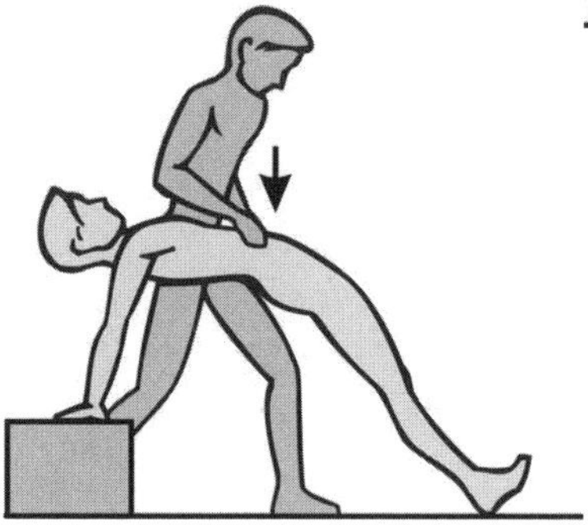

Fig. 28.54. Same as Fig.28.48, support on the box

Fig. 28.55. Same as Fig. 28.49, holding one arm in the air

Fig. 28.56. Same as Fig. 28.50, arms on the box

Fig. 28.57. Same as Fig. 28.51, one arm on the box

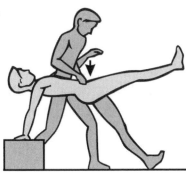

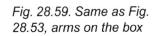

Fig. 28.58. Same as Fig. 28.52, one arm on the box

Fig. 28.59. Same as Fig. 28.53, arms on the box

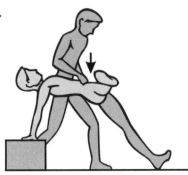

Fig. 28.60. Same as
Fig.28.48, feet on the box

Fig. 28.61. Arms on the
box, feet on the floor,
move hips up & down

Fig. 28.62. Same as
Fig. 28.61, one arm
support on the box

Fig. 28.63. Same as Fig.
28.61, one leg in the air

186

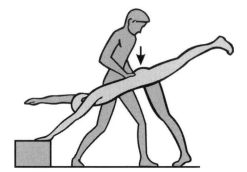

Fig. 28.64. Same as Fig. 28.61, one arm & the opposite leg in the air

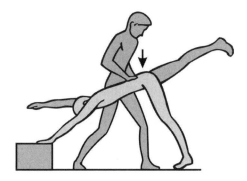

Fig. 28.65. Same as Fig. 28.61, one arm & the same side leg in the air

Fig. 28.66. Same as Fig. 28.61, one leg held to the side

187

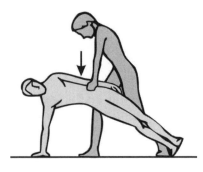

Fig. 28.67. One arm, two feet on the floor, move hips up & down

Fig. 28.68. One arm & foot on the floor, the top leg held in the air, move hips up & down

Fig. 28.69. Same as Fig.28.68, the bottom leg held in the air

Chapter 29

EXERCISES FOR HAMSTRINGS

The largest muscles in the body, the hamstrings are the workhorses of the runner. Responsible for releasing the body from support and allowing it to free fall, they work harder than any other muscles while you are running and must be properly prepared, not only to perform well, but also to avoid injury. The best exercises for the hamstrings are the ones that most closely resemble the kinesthetic and dynamic characteristics of running technique.

Hamstring exercises performed on machines (Figs. 29.1-29.3) are the easiest to master because they make no requirement of you to achieve balance and integration of movements with the rest of the body. At the same time, they are very safe because it is quite easy to regulate the amount of resistance simply by selecting the amount of weight with which you will work. For those very reasons, however, they are the most limited in value, because balance and integration are vital in perfect running. These exercises are recommended at the outset of your program and should be mastered before you move onto the next level.

189

On Machines

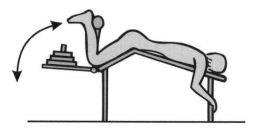

Fig. 29.1. Curl the legs

Fig. 29.2. Curl the legs

*Fig. 29.3. Standing
on one leg, curl
the other one*

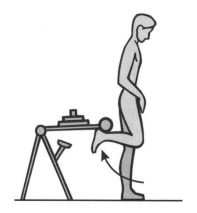

When you work with free weights (Figs. 29.4-29.6), you assume responsibility for the speed, balance and direction of the movement. This forces you to once again make micro-corrections and thus focuses your strength development of perfect movement. This becomes even more apparent as the form of resistance switches to stretch cords (Figs. 29.7-29.19) where there is active resistance trying to remove you from perfect balance. By working against this resistance, you heighten your proprioceptive awareness and your ability to stay in perfect balance against forceful resistance.

With Free Weights

Fig. 29.4. Balance on one leg on the box, pull the airborne ankle with weight vertically under the hip

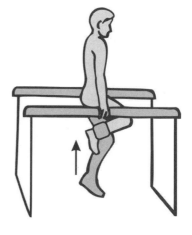

Fig. 29.5. Support on parallel bars, pull the airborne foot with the ankle weight vertically under the hip

191

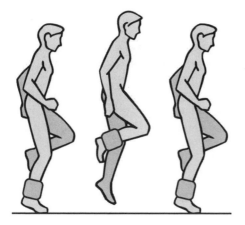

Fig. 29.6. Hop in place or forward in the running pose, with the ankle weight on the support foot, by pulling the foot up from the ground

In Lying Position with Stretch Cords

Fig. 29.7. Lying face down, curl the leg tied at the ankle to the rubber band

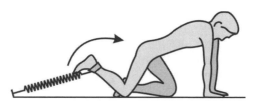

Fig. 29.8. Support on hands and knees, curl the leg

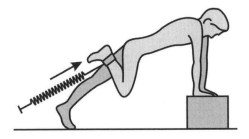

Fig. 29.9. Support on the box, pull the ankle towards the hip

Fig. 29.10. Support on the elbows, pull the leg towards the hip

Fig. 29.11. Support on the elbows, curl the leg and return it upwards

Fig. 29.12. Support on the arms, hips in the air, curl the leg under the hip

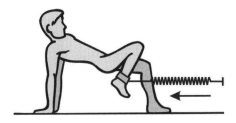

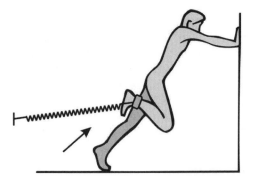

Fig. 29.13. Leaning towards the wall, tap the foot tied with the rubber band at the ankle

Fig. 29.14. In the front lunge, with the rubber band pulling the ankle forward, raise the foot under the hips

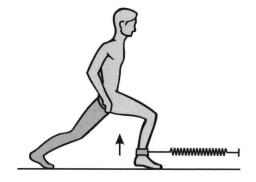

Fig. 29.15. Same as Fig. 29.14, with the rubber band pulling the front foot back

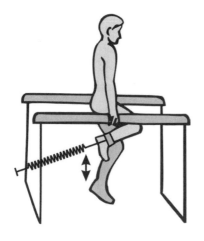

Fig. 29.16. Support on parallel bars, with the legs airborne, and the rubber band tied to the ankle, pull the foot under the hip

Fig. 29.17. In the running pose, with the rubber bands on both ankles, change support by pulling the support foot up

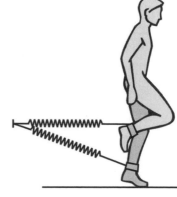

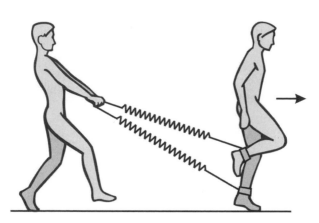

Fig. 29.18. With the partner behind, holding the rubber bands tied to the ankles, change support by moving forward

195

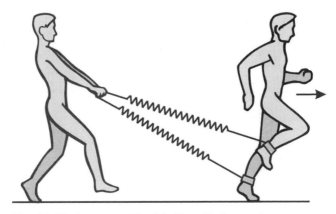

Fig. 29.19. Same as Fig. 29.18, with the partner regulating the rubber bands' resistance, start running

As with the hips exercises, the hamstring exercises with partner's resistance (Figs. 29.20-29.21) allow your partner to both give you resistance and guide you toward perfect movement. This "intelligent" resistance can be the final difference as you hone your movements and build your strength.

Fig. 29.20. Move the ankle up and down

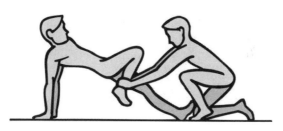

Fig. 29.21. Move the ankle back and forth

197

Chapter 30

*Force without wisdom
falls of its own weight.*
Horace

INTEGRATING STRENGTH CONDITIONING INTO YOUR TRAINING PROGRAM

While it is clear that specific strength training is an essential component of a balanced approach to running, you must be careful to use this training in the right way for the right reasons. Basically, there are three categories of strength training: Development, Maintenance and Recovery. You can use any given exercise for any of these three categories; the difference will come in the intensity and number of repetitions (reps) performed.

In general, the development phase involves the greatest volume of work, in number of sets, intensity and difficulty. The maintenance phase sees reductions in the numbers of sets and/or reps and the recovery phase involves reductions in intensity and difficulty, with an increase in sets and/or reps.

The development phase of strength conditioning actually refers to two different circumstances. If you are a runner doing strength conditioning for the very first time, development must be approached cautiously as you learn the exercises and adapt to the new stresses being placed on your body. So while "development" implies the greatest volume of work, you should allow several months of adaptation before attempting high volumes of intensity and difficulty.

From that point on, as you move through the phases of maintenance and recovery and then cycle back to development, you can be more comfortable moving into more intense work. However, if you abandon strength conditioning for any significant time, consider yourself to be back to square one and incorporate a slow build-up into your program.

Generally speaking, when you are in the development phase of strength conditioning, you should set aside time for two to three sessions a week that are exclusively dedicated to strength conditioning. As you move into maintenance, you can incorporate the strength session into another workout. Finally, when you are in a period of your greatest running mileage or intensity, you should schedule your strength conditioning at the conclusion of your running workouts. In this case, the objective of the conditioning is return your muscular functions to normal and to minimize the tension and soreness generated by extremely hard running training.

In the development phase, each of your two to three sessions per week should be focused on a specific area of the body. One session should focus on your legs, one on your upper body and one on the lower back and abdominals. The workout for the legs should be scheduled with a recovery day in mind, so that your legs have an opportunity to benefit from the strength gains before being forced to work out again on the road or track.

Remember: the key word here is "development." All too often runners think of a rest day as a wasted day, a day when they could have been training. Don't fall into this trap. A rest day is a day that allows the gains from a particular workout or series of workouts to be consolidated into your body. If you don't give your body the time to recover and instead keep pushing it from day to day, you won't receive optimum benefit from your efforts and will ultimately break down. Rest and recovery are every bit as important as training.

In the development period, your number of reps within a given set can go as high as ten, performed with increasing intensity. Depending on the particular exercise, you can do anywhere from one to five sets, with five being appropriate for some of the jumping exercises.

Think your way through these sets, concentrating on the feelings in your body. During the development cycle, you should exercise to the point where you are feeling significant tension in the muscle groups being exercised, but don't push to the point of muscular failure. After a while you will begin to recognize your own boundaries, even as you see your capabilities increase.

As you make the transition to the maintenance phase, it is still best to devote one weekly session to each area of the body as you did during development, but now these strength sessions can be incorporated into a running workout. For example, you can schedule the turn-around point in a 10K run to be at a spot where it is comfortable to perform some jumping exercises. Stop at the turnaround, recover for a few minutes, and then do your jumps.

Since you are now in the maintenance period, don't put as much intensity into the jumps as you did during development. You can keep the reps around ten, but hold the sets of each exercise to no more than three. You may also want to limit the number of different exercises you do during a session and vary the exercises from session to session.

In the same way, you can plan a run through a local Vita-Course park to do your upper-body work or find a spot conducive to working your lower back and abdominals. By integrating your strength sessions into a run, you not only free up some time in your overall life schedule, but you bring real focus into your running sessions. Instead of just slogging through the miles you had planned for the day, your workout unfolds with a much greater interest level. You run the first half with a nice tempo, whip through some quick exercises and then real focus on bringing it all together with a faster tempo on the return route. Your sense of purpose should benefit substantially from the combined sessions.

Finally, you reach racing season. This is where your strength sessions contribute to recovery of your muscle groups. Generally speaking, during racing season you will be running fewer miles during the week, but one or two of your sessions will be conducted at a very high intensity level. This is when you move your "strength" sessions to the end of your running workouts and use them to cool down your body and return your muscles to normal operation.

If you simply stop after a very high intensity run and head to the showers, your muscles will still be quivering, your nerve endings will be firing and your overworked metabolism won't want to just shut down immediately. To ease the transition from intense workout to normal life, you need to combine easy walking with your exercises, now performed with a very light touch in relatively high volumes.

Whereas you were approaching muscular failure with your exercises during the development phase, you now want to feel just the opposite. Really tune into the feedback your body is generating and feel the recovery take place into your muscles and connective tissue. It is vastly better to recover while you are still in your running gear than it is to make a quick progression from the run to the shower to the couch. Active recovery trumps a prone "crash" every time.

And don't forget to do your walk-off and recovery exercises after your races, too. While it is quite tempting to head for the fruit table and quickly progress to those hard-earned beers that are offered at so many races, but first take the time to take care of your body.

In the big picture, the development phase should be considered your "pre-season" preparation, the maintenance phase would be "early season" and recovery would be devoted to "peak season", but there are no hard and fast rules about this, because our lives, and our training, rarely stay so neatly packaged. Use your own judgment about when to use each phase and make adjustments to your schedule as needed, particularly if injuries or "life issues" take you out of your normal training pattern.

You may even find that the two races you have pointed to are at the beginning and end of the summer. In this case it makes sense to reach a peak for the first race, and then go back to the development phase of your strength conditioning for four to six weeks before you begin to sharpen for your second target race.

The ultimate point is this: if you're really serious about improving your running performance, don't think of strength conditioning as something "extra" or a luxury for which you don't have the heart or the time. Strength conditioning is an integral part of running training, a necessity that is every bit as important as piling up the miles on the road or track.

Chapter 31

RUNNING ON SAND

To the millions of landlocked runners worldwide, there are few more "romantic" visions than running on the beach. There is something primeval and satisfying about running at the interface of land and sea and the reward of a pleasant cooling-off dip afterwards is a well-earned pleasure. But take note; depending on the consistency and pitch of the sand on the particular beach of your dreams, sand running can be one of the hardest things you'll ever do (Fig. 31.1).

Fig. 31.1. Sand running

Hard pack sand, like the type that allows safe passage of cars on "The World's Most Famous Beach", Daytona Beach, Florida, is a relative rarity. It's more likely that you'll find yourself in deeper, less compact sand. While this can be incredibly difficult, it is also very useful in mastering the art of the Pose Method of Running. Running on sand strengthens the muscles and ligaments, develops muscular balance in the legs, stabilizes your joints and develops aerobic capacity. Perhaps most importantly, sand running hones your skills of interacting with the ground.

Many of the benefits of sand running derive from the fact that it is a relatively unstable surface. When you are running on the sand, your feet may sink in, slide in any direction and be far more difficult to release from support. These conditions force you to learn the best way to interact with support and approach optimal running technique.

Additionally, the difficulty of running on sand makes it virtually impossible to overstride. If you are having problems breaking the habits of either pushing off with your foot on take-off or landing on the heel and rolling through to the mid-foot to the toes, you'll find sand running a very effective tool in getting the "feel" of proper running technique. Trying to run in that old style, you'll find that you quickly bog down. However, if you run with the light touch and short strides of the Pose Method, you won't penetrate nearly as far into the sand and you'll move along much more rapidly.

The learning curve will increase even faster if you do your sand running barefoot. The far smaller surface area of your foot as opposed to a running shoe will put a premium on proper technique to avoid sinking deeper into the sand. Further, eliminating the big dead layers of shoes and socks will vastly increase the feedback you get from your feet. By increasing your kinesthetic awareness of what is going on beneath you will make it easier to correct mistakes and improve your technique.

Sand running can be very difficult. In your initial attempts, you would be wise not to treat it as a "run" in the common vernacular, but as an exercise or drill to support your running. Don't expect to measure your sand runs in the conventional sense of time or distance but instead as contributors to your overall mastery of running technique and strength development. Expect some serious soreness in your calves and quads, but realize that such soreness is an indication of ongoing strength development. Expect, as well, some serious huffing and puffing. It can be downright discouraging to head out for a run on the sand only to slow to a halt within minutes, if not seconds, as you come to terms with just how tough it is. But, as with the muscular soreness, that huffing and puffing is telling you that serious work is being done that will be of significant benefit to your cardio-vascular and respiratory systems.

At the beginning, you'll probably do several short runs on the sand punctuated by somewhat exhausted walks. It's best to run only until you feel it impossible to maintain proper running technique, rather than keep going as your technique utterly disintegrates. As your overall technique improves and your strength becomes greater, you can vary your approach to sand running, mixing in longer runs with tempo runs, short intervals or even sprints. Depending on your personal proximity to a satisfactory area for sand running, you can run in sand as often as twice a week or make it a special "treat" a few times a year. Or you may pick a particular period of the year when you run frequently on the sand and then lay off on it for several months.

You might even become a sand connoisseur, running the extremely challenging dunes of the Outer Banks of North Carolina, seeking out the almost bottomless sugar sand of Central Florida or crunching you way across the pebbly beaches of Northern California. After all, there's nothing wrong with aesthetically enjoying your runs, even as you work as hard as you possibly can.

There is one caveat about sand running that should be mentioned. Among its primary benefits are muscular balance and strengthening of connective tissue. Take note that many beaches have somewhat severe slopes leading toward the water. Running only one direction on these beaches can ultimately lead your body to subconsciously correct for this uneven terrain, which can in turn lead to debilitating injuries. Make sure to balance this out by running both directions or moving further away from the water where the slope is less severe.

Chapter 32

UPHILL AND DOWNHILL RUNNING

Even for those who have never run a step, the words "Heartbreak Hill" conjure up an indelible image of the indomitable spirit of humans trying to overcome the challenges of nature. Hills are as much as part of the running experience as running shoes, singlets and the euphoric feeling known as the "runner's high."

Many are the runners who plan routes to avoid beastly inclines; far fewer are those who recognize hills as opportunities for improvement and development. With few exceptions, the latter class contains the better runners. As a quantifiable, repeatable, unyielding challenge, a good hill is a constant in a changing world, a reality check for those who have deluded themselves into thinking they are faster or fitter than they really are.

And for the runner who is seeking to master the Pose Method of Running, hills also represent big question marks. "How do I run in the Pose Method when I'm going up or down hills?" is a FAQ of the highest order. What seems so simple on flat land becomes vexing as the pitch of the road or trail changes.

Running uphill, in particular, seems to defy the logic of the Pose Method, which relies on tapping the power of gravity to generate forward motion (Fig. 32.1). If I'm running against gravity, you may ask, how can I *use* gravity to go forward while going up a hill? A valid question, and for the answer we head into the woods and turn to the fine art of tree cutting.

Fig. 32.1. Uphill running

If you've ever had to clear a hillside, you'll have encountered a similar problem. To wit, how do you chop down a tree and have it fall *up* the hill? Logic would seem to tell you that a chopped tree is going to fall down the hill, way down the hill. Actually, though, it's a simple matter to drop the tree wherever you want it. The first thing you do is take a hatchet and chop a notch near the base of the tree on the side where you want it to fall. Once you have a nice deep notch pointed right where you want it to fall, you go to the other side of the tree and begin chopping or sawing slightly above, and down toward, the notch.

As the line of your cut reaches the notch, the collective weight of the tree will lean on the gap created by the notch and – timberrrrr! – the tree falls right where you want it. It couldn't be easier.

The same principle applies to running uphill. As you run in the Pose Method, you always have a slight, barely perceptible, forward lean to your body. As you release your foot from support, you are, in effect, creating a notch between the weight of your body and the direction in which you want to head. The momentum of your running plus the forward lean allows gravity to continue to work for you – you literally free fall uphill.

This is not to say that running uphill becomes an easy task. You still are subject to the physics involved of moving your body mass in a direction opposed to gravity, but at least you're using gravity to help you along the way.

The value of uphill running in mastering the Pose Method and building strength now becomes obvious. In order to continue moving up the hill, you're going to have to maintain or even increase your cadence, which in turn mandates short strides. This means your hamstrings are going to be doing an awful lot of work, quick, explosive work. The faster they release from support on the earth, the less load of body weight they will have to bear.

This work really calls your muscular elasticity into play while at the same time builds a greater sensory perception of releasing your foot from support. Just as significantly, once you truly understand how to run uphill, it becomes an important weapon in your mental arsenal. Hills no longer represent barriers, but become opportunities to exploit your technique to advantage against your opponents.

All of this sounds great, you think, but what about the downhills (Fig. 32.2)? After all, many veterans of the Boston Marathon say that it's not going *up* Heartbreak Hill, but going back *down*, that does all the damage. Probably the most dangerous thing about running downhill

Fig. 32.2. Downhill running

is that it seems easy. After suffering to get to the top of the hill, the natural reaction is to relax and enjoy the ride as you go back down.

Of course, what happens is that your stride lengthens, you add a little bounce to it and you end up landing with a big thud with every footfall (Fig. 32.3). This sends a tremendous shock all the way up your spine and generally pounds every joint in your body while sending distress signals to your muscles and connective tissue.
Something has to happen to arrest the speed of your descent and the quads take up the challenge. Suddenly you're in a braking mode that can rapidly become a *breaking* mode as what at first

seemed a respite becomes punishment. No wonder the last six or so miles into Boston are so brutal.

Managing the challenge of downhill running is accomplished first

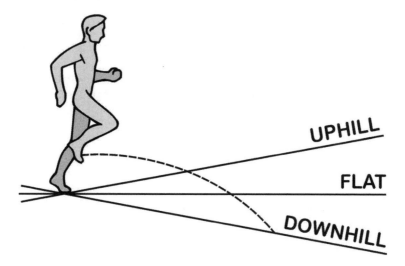

Fig. 32.3. The difference in stride length while running uphill, flat and downhill depends on the degree of inclination of the surface. In downhill it's the longest, in uphill – the shortest

by continuing to pay attention to what you're doing, resisting the temptation to take a mental holiday. Keep your strides short and low to the ground. Any excess vertical oscillation just increases the havoc gravity can cause on your body, so by all means don't "bounce." Don't let your feet drift out in front you; keep landing directly under your body. And don't let your body get away from you by falling too fast. Stay erect and minimize forward lean. That way you'll remove the pounding from your legs and descend in a controlled fashion rather than resembling a runaway freight train.

From a sensory standpoint, the greatest value of downhill running in your training program is that it really tunes you in to the concept of letting your feet drop back to support rather than forcing them down. Running on flat ground it is difficult to get a sense for whether you are pushing your feet down or just letting them drop, but going downhill really helps you focus on the relaxation necessary for the foot drop. One you get the feeling that gravity really will put your foot right where it needs to go, you can transfer that feeling to flat running and save yourself a lot of energy.

As with other special strength conditioning, how much hill running you incorporate into your training will in large part be determined by where you live. Flatlanders often use bridges, overpasses or stadium steps to get their hill work while mountain dwellers often beg for just a patch of flat land so they avoid the constant up and down.

Whatever your own circumstances may be, no training week is complete without at least one hill session. Start out with short efforts where you concentrate entirely on form until you're confident that you're carrying your Pose Method technique with you both up and down the hills. As you master the technique, you can add both longer and faster efforts into your repertoire until you become a virtual mountain goat – at which point you can go look for a truly nasty 10K or trail run to display your newly earned skills.

Chapter 33

TRAIL RUNNING

Trail running may be the purest form of running there is. On the trail, you channel Phidippides, you are a hunter/gatherer, you are one with nature (Fig. 33.1). Free of pavement, distanced from cars

Fig. 33.1. Trail running

and their noxious fumes, and tuned in to the scents and sights of the forest or desert, you have the sense of going somewhere, rather than just running. Trail running takes the drudgery out of running and replaces it with a sense of adventure. We should all be so lucky as to have beautiful trails just out the back door.

Aside from benefiting the soul, trail running is also exceptionally good for the body. While road running generally provides a very uniform and stable surface, on the trail things are generally very uneven, with twists and turns, rocks and roots and frequent ups and downs. In other words, trail running is full of unpredictable support conditions, and therefore entails specific requirements for success. Mastery of trail running includes very short stride length, high cadence, and an acutely developed sense of feel. In order to continually adapt to changing trail conditions and directions, you need to be extraordinarily light on your feet and stay relaxed rather than tensing up.

Consequently, the time spent on support should be very short, and landing should be done cautiously, with the foot always ready to be quickly removed from the ground, should uneven trail conditions so require. This mandates that your landing be on the forefoot and that your muscular elasticity is fully developed, ready for the quick actions that can mean the difference between safe passage and a sprained or broken ankle.

This kind of running with constantly changing conditions promotes the development of a very flexible and reactive system of body movements and trains your neuromuscular system to be ready for every kind of situation you might encounter.

There are some more subtle physical benefits to trail running as well. On the road, where you are able to more perfectly control the exactness of each footfall, you end up with what you might call very linear development of your muscles and connective tissue. You will get very strong while moving directly straight ahead, but you will not be conditioned to absorb the impact of an unexpected misstep caused by a pothole, a branch in the road or even loose rocks.

216

In contrast, the very unevenness of the trail leads to a more well-rounded development of your muscles, ligaments, tendons and joints. By teaching the body, legs and feet to land on the ground at any angle, position, pitch or consistency, trail running builds the comprehensive strength that will help to keep you injury free. Simultaneously, it is also a very good psychological training which prepares you to be ready for quick reactions to any changes in running conditions without becoming unsettled or distracted.

As with sand and hill running, where you live will dictate just how much trail running you can incorporate into your training plan. If good trails are readily accessible, there is nothing wrong with making trail running the mainstay of your program, with relatively infrequent jaunts on surfaces like macadam or concrete. In you require a longer drive to get to your favorite trail, you might use it as your long weekend run, which will give you a welcome psychological break from the normal day-to-day routine even as it helps strengthen your body.

In short, no running program is complete without the occasional trail run and the more you can work into your routine, the better off you will be.

Chapter 34

RUNNING BAREFOOT

While the evolution of the modern running shoe may be a wonderful thing (and they're certainly a vast improvement over the thin-soled track spikes some of us wore in the 60s and 70s) they may also bring with them some problems. Read the ads and you'll see hype touting things like comfort, stability and – inevitably – heel cushioning. They all sound like pretty wonderful attributes until you recognize that they may add up to nothing more than artificial means to disguise the effects of poor technique.

Even worse, in the case of the built-up heels, they may actually promote poor technique. By now, you should recognize that proper running technique involves landing on the forefoot, not on the heel. Truth is, landing on the heel *should* hurt, because that's not the way humans were designed to run. But put a big, fat cushion on the back end of a running shoe and not only will your heels not hurt when you run, it will be hard not to land there, because there's so much mass in the way.

Take off your shoes (Fig. 34.1), though, and you'll quickly realize that landing on your heels is just not a very smart way for swiftly moving humans to transport themselves across significant distances. Take even a short run and you'll quickly move towardthe Pose Method, taking shorter strides and landing on the forefoot.

Interestingly, if you study the running form of the fantastically successful African runners who have dominated the world distance scene for much of the past four decades and you'll see solid Pose-style running form. This running form was not intuitive, nor was it the result of good coaching. In most cases, it resulted from the childhood efforts of a continent of runners who had no shoes. Barefoot running showed them the way to proper technique.

Like most Western world citizens who have literally worn shoes since birth, you're probably a serious tenderfoot, so you're not likely to go out and run a marathon sans shoes, as did Ethiopia's Abebe Bikila in winning the 1960 Olympic marathon in Rome. However, there are plenty of benefits to be gained by starting out gingerly with some barefoot running exercises (1).

Fig. 34.1. Barefoot running

On the physical side, barefoot running will help develop local strength around the ankles and feet. Stability shouldn't come from the artificial means of a wide-platform shoe, but from strong muscles, joints and connective tissue. Developing this strength, instead of buying it, will greatly reduce your chances of being sidelined by Achilles tendonitis, plantar fasciitis or other common runners' injuries.

It stands to reason that the proper alignment of the entire body flows from proper foot placement during the landing phase of the stride. Land with the foot too far in front of the body, off-center, or on the heel, and your whole body will be out of alignment. Barefoot running, which pretty much forces you to land on your forefoot, goes a long way toward setting up proper alignment from the feet all the way to the crown of your head.

Now things are starting to come together. You're landing on your forefoot, your body is in perfect alignment and you're building strength and stability in and around your feet. What comes next? Why muscular elasticity and reduced time spent on support, of course. When you're running barefoot, you don't even have to conjure up an image of running on hot coals to make sure you pick up your feet as quickly as they touch the ground. You'll tap the ground with a quick, light touch and pick your foot right back up again. In short, run barefoot and you'll run using the Pose Method in no time.

As with all other special strength and conditioning exercises for the Pose Method, you'll want to start your Pose Method running in small doses. In fact, you may even want to start off with some barefoot walking, just to build up a little layer of callous on the bottoms of your feet.

The best places to start barefoot running are either on sand or a good composition running track. In either case there's relatively little chance of something sharp and nasty doing serious damage to your tender feet and you can get excellent feedback that tells you where your foot is landing. Sand will be more effective in building strength, while the track will help you be more precise.

Start out with repeats of as little as 25 yards as you seek to find proper form, then graduate to slightly longer distances once you're comfortable running barefoot. Remember that your main objectives in this exercise are to develop strength and control, not endurance, so don't worry if a barefoot session doesn't tally the kind of mileage that looks good in your training log. In fact, at the beginning you can do your barefoot drills on a "rest" day.

Down the road – way down the road – you may want to consider trail running barefoot. It sounds daunting, but the well-conditioned foot is perfectly capable of cruising along a good trail for mile after mile, perfectly in tune with nature. In fact, the co-author of this book once completed the final 10K of a 15K running leg in a triathlon barefoot...in Georgia...on asphalt...in the blazing heat of summer. The only injuries suffered were the blisters that caused the shoes to be discarded in the first place.

1. Robbins, S.E. and Hanna, A.M., 1987, Running-related injury prevention through barefoot adaptations. Med, and Science in Sports and Exercise, 19:148-156.

Chapter 35

DEVELOPING FLEXIBILITY

If you're planning to race a car or a bicycle, you'll no doubt want to use a "well-oiled machine." It's just common sense: you'll want everything lubricated and in perfect running order in order to achieve an optimum performance and avoid mechanical failure that could lead to wrecks. However, when most of us go out to run, we're operating "vehicles" that are anything but "well-oiled machines". Face it, as runners, most of us are either young, and therefore self-considered to be indestructible, or verging on old, and resigned to making the best of what we have.

Either way, by failing to oil our running machines, we not only run slower than we should, but we also greatly increase our chances of suffering running-related injuries that will most definitely lead to diminished performance and in many cases, may cause up to give up the sport entirely. It's no secret that the ranks of swimmers, cyclists and rowers are filled with former runners who believe that their bodies are no longer up to the challenge of running. The sad thing is that they have given up their cherished sport in the belief that running itself was the culprit, when in fact they could have continued running forever if they had only adopted proper technique and kept their bodies flexible.

There are two principle factors that keep runners from giving proper time and effort to developing enhanced flexibility. The first is the failure to make the connection between flexibility and performance. Runners are nothing if not pragmatic and are prone not to waste effort on something they don't believe will help their performance.

The second factor is time. With the speed of contemporary life, it is no small challenge to carve out 'x' number of hours to devote to running. For most runners, the equation is simple: time spent stretching is time not spent running, which equals slower, not faster running. Besides, most runners are runners because they like to run. If they use up their "free" time doing something that is not running, well, it's not hard to see that, as wasted time. Running, as a habit, is indeed a jealous mistress.

But time spent "oiling the body" is far from wasted time, any more than the time a racecar spends in the garage is wasted time. Preparing your body to run is vital not only to enhancing your performance, but also to ensuring that you will be able to run happily and injury-free all of your life.

Before going into details, a couple of examples are in order. Floridian Kelly Slater is a six-time world champion surfer. At 29, he had been "retired" for two or three years, but headed back onto the circuit in 2002 in search of his seventh world title. To chase the title, he'll spend much of his year in airplanes as he competes in Australia, South Africa, Europe, South America, the United States, the South Pacific and, ultimately, Hawaii. The travel alone is brutal on the body, not to mention the pounding absorbed in some of the largest rideable waves on the planet.

Yet Slater pays so much attention to taking care of his body that Outside Magazine reported that he's "a yoga teacher's dream: He can lie on his stomach and pull his feet flat to the floor beside his head" (1). At first you may dismiss this particular ability as that of a "freak of nature," a particular quirk of someone who has mastered a balance sport. But don't forget that we have now defined running as a balance sport, one that requires total control for success.

You may never equal the pretzel logic of a Kelly Slater, but being flexible is certainly a component of athletic success.

For an example closer to running, consider the case of Lance Armstrong. Most people are aware of his cancer comeback story and the changes he made in his cycling style (as mentioned previously in this book) that transformed him from a powerful one-day racer into the world's dominant stage racer. In fact, after he won the Tour de France back-to-back in 1999 and 2000, most people were left asking a simple question, "How could he possibly get any better?"

In his preparation for the 2001 Tour, he answered that question by adding an entirely new component to his regimen: an hour a day of stretching. The results were evident when he won the Tour of Switzerland and the Tour de France back-to-back in absolutely dominant fashion. Stretching not only improved his strength and power, but also helped him recover, a vital concern in stage racing. Over five weeks of intense racing at the highest level of the sport through June and July 2001, he never suffered a single bad day. By never showing weakness, he simply showed his competitors that they had no chance whatsoever to defeat him.

But what is it about flexibility that makes it so critical to athletic performance? There are really three components to human flexibility: mobility in the joints, elasticity in the ligaments and tendons, and relaxation in the muscles (Fig. 35.1).

Fig.35.1.Flexibility & Running

Starting with the joints, the age-old plaint, "Oh, my aching bones" really refers to your joints. When you wake up in the morning feeling like a truck ran over you and the idea of touching your toes seems as remote as the notion that you might become President, it's your joints that just aren't lubed and functioning properly. And no wonder, since most of us accept creaking joints as a condition of ageing and not the result of neglect. But, thankfully, neglect it is, which means we can do a lot to restore full mobility to our joints.

And why wouldn't we? Just as we wouldn't want to drive a car or ride a bike where every moving part squeaked relentlessly, why would we want to run with a sack full of joints that were creaky and painful?

Operating in close coordination with the joints are the all-important ligaments, cartilage and tendons, the connective tissue that acts as a buffer between the joints, bones, and muscles, keeping the whole operation running smoothly. As mobility is the prime consideration in the joints, elasticity is paramount in the connective tissue. Without sufficient elasticity, the connective tissue forfeits its role as a buffer and shifts the mechanical load of performance to the joints, bones and muscles, reducing performance and increasing the risk of injury.

Since they work together so closely, it makes sense to address the needs of the joints and connective tissue together. The overriding concept is simple: there are no unimportant parts in the human body. While we have identified the hamstring as the workhorse of running, every single fiber of your body comes into play during peak performance and must be prepared accordingly. From the smallest joint to the largest muscle, everything must receive attention.

As we consider the value of exercising our joints and connective tissue, it's worth bearing in mind that the best runners look smooth and effortless when they are performing at their very best. It stands to reason that smooth, effortless performance cannot be achieved with creaky joints and stiff connective tissue. And while nature may bless some of us with greater flexibility, all of

226

Fig. 35.2. Hold your fingers and pull them down to stretch your hands

and unbend them, stretch them, get them moving. Don't hurry through the process, take the time to feel that each joint is becoming more flexible, let the heat of your hand flow into the joints.

Then continue moving through the body, making sure that all your joints and the surrounding connective tissue are manipulated, stretched and warmed. You'll find that it feels surprisingly good to get everything opened up and moving. In all likelihood, you'll soon wonder how you ever ran without engaging in this little routine.

us can vastly improve our own flexibility with just a modest amount of attention.

Mobility exercises for the joints begin with the fingers (Figs. 35.2-35.10) and flow through the hands, wrists, elbows, shoulders, vertebrae, hips, knees, ankles and all the way to the toes. These exercises are very basic and don't take up much time. Essentially you're promoting mobility by moving the joints in every direction. Twist your finger joints, bend

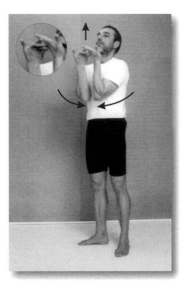

Fig. 35.3. Clinch your fingers in front of the chest, with palms turned up, and stretch the fingers and palms by moving elbows together

227

Fig. 35.4. With clinched
fingers & palms facing
outward, straighten the
arms in front of the chest

Fig. 35.5. Arms in front
of the chest, and elbows
sideways, push your fingers
together and stretch them

228

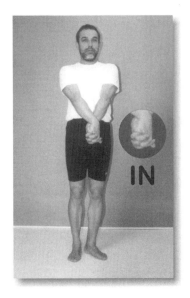 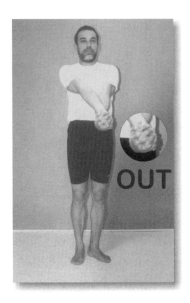

Fig. 35.6 a & b. Arms in front, hands crossed, and fingers clenched, rotate hands in & out twisting the wrists and hands

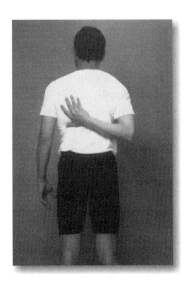

Fig. 35.7. Hand behind the back, touch the opposite shoulder blade

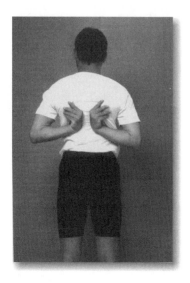

Fig. 35.8. Both hands behind the back, touch the shoulders blades

Fig. 35.9. Touching your fingers behind the back

Fig. 35.10. Palms together with fingers up behind the back ("praying")

The process of working on your joints and connective tissue is both local and complex. On the one hand, you should work on specific joints; on the other you should focus on exercises that integrate systems of joints and connective tissue to make sure that they work well in concert together (Figs. 35.11-35.25). Study the illustrated examples for routines that are effective.

231

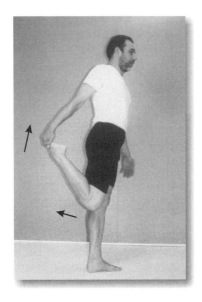

Fig. 35.11. Balance on one leg, holding the other behind, pull your toes to the hips

Fig. 35.12. Balance on one leg, holding the other behind, bend forward touching the ground with the other hand

Fig. 35.13. Front lunge, bounce up & down

Fig. 35.14. Deep front lunge, bend forward touching the ground with your forearms and elbows

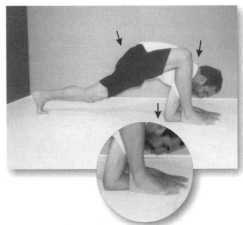

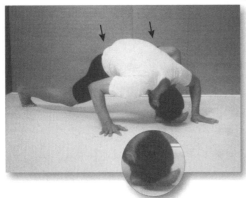

Fig. 35.15. Same as 35.14, hands on the floor, touching the front foot with your forehead

233

Fig. 35.16.
Sideway deep
squat, shift the
body weight from
one leg to the
other

Fig. 35.17.
Sideway deep
squat, bend
forward with your
arms stretched
on the floor

Fig. 35.18.
Deep squat
on one leg,
bend forward
to the stretched
leg, touch the
knee with your
forehead and
the toes with
the opposite
hand

Fig. 35.19. Legs bent and crossed, bend forward stretching the arms

Fig. 35.20. Same as Fig. 35.19, hands on the thighs, bend forward touching the floor with your forehead

Fig. 35.21. Legs bent, feet held together, bend forward touching the toes with your forehead

235

Fig. 35.22. Legs in the hurdler's position, hands holding feet, bend forward touching the floor with your forehead

Fig. 35.23. One leg bent, the other crossed over it, bend forward touching the front foot with your forehead and stretching the same side arm on the floor

Fig. 35.24. One leg on the floor, hold the other foot with both hands and straighten it up, touching the knee with your forehead

Fig. 35.25. Balance with legs held straight in the air, arms around the thighs, touch your knees with your forehead

It may seem somewhat of a contradiction in terms that the ability of muscles to perform work is dependent on their ability to relax, but again think back to the vision of smooth and effortless performance. Relaxed muscles bring about smooth performance; tense muscles engender jerky movement and poor performance. For a visual picture, think of the super slow-motion video you've seen of Olympic sprinters. In those images, the sprinters' muscles appear to be more liquid than solid, swinging freely like jelly despite the enormous efforts being made. By contrast, sprinters who are not relaxed are the ones who end up tearing their hamstrings and writhing in agony on the track.

But how can you relax your muscles when you're trying your hardest? The answer to that question is the key to peak performance. Muscles perform work by extending and contracting. If a muscle is not relaxed at full extension, it has a tendency to tear or snap, hence the image of the runner writhing on the track. So, a muscle can only effectively extend as far as it remains relaxed. The instant extension exceeds relaxation bad things happen.

So it is really a key component of your training and not agratuitous add-on to systematically prepare your muscles for relaxation at full extension. There are a number of strategies to achieve muscular flexibility and relaxation.

Before you break out the yoga mat or the free weights, you'll be interested to know that the first element of muscular flexibility is purely psychological, built on psycho-muscular relaxation techniques. Used widely in psychotherapy, the techniques call on you to concentrate on sensations of heaviness, warmth and relaxation in separate muscles and muscle groups. First developed by J. H. Shultz in the 1920s, these exercises of mental imagery have a real effect on developing a greater degree of flexibility in your muscles (2).

Moving into the physical realm, the next set of exercises involves maintaining a fully extended static fixed position of specific muscles or muscle groups (Figs. 35.26-35.37). Whether you call this simple stretching or yoga, the idea is to achieve full extension and then hold that position for an extended period of time. This is a progressive exercise: in a given session each time you perform a given stretch you should achieve slightly improved extension and over time your extension should improve substantially.

Fig. 35.26. Feet apart along the sagittal lane, bend forward with hands touching the ground

Fig. 35.27. Same as Fig. 35.26, with feet together along the sagittal line

Fig. 35.28. One foot on the heel in front of the other, with toes up, bend forward touching the ground

Fig. 35.29. Heels together, with toes up, bend forward touching the ground

Fig. 35.30. Feet flat, with legs crossed, bend forward touching the ground

Fig. 35.31. Feet on the lateral side, with legs crossed, bend forward touching the ground

Fig. 35.32. Feet along the sagittal line, the front foot on the lateral side, bend forward touching the ground

Fig. 35.33. Both feet on the lateral side, bend forward touching the ground

Fig. 35.34. Feet together, arms straightened behind, hands clenched together, bend forward touching the knees with your forehead

Fig. 35.35. Heels together, with toes pointing out, bend forward touching the ground

Fig. 35.36. Feet pointing outward, one in front of the other, bend forward touching the ground

Fig. 35.37. Feet wide apart, hands holding the ankles, bend forward touching the floor with your head

243

The simple toe touch (aka "The Hands to Feet Pose') is a great example. If you haven't been in the habit of touching your toes on a regular basis, you may find it shockingly difficult to make it even to your ankles on your first try. And it could well be even harder to hold the position at the ankles for more than a couple of seconds. By the third or fourth try in your first session, you may make it closer to your toes and be able to stay there for ten or more seconds. After a couple of weeks of regular stretching, you should be able to put your palms flat on the ground and maintain the position for more than thirty seconds.

This is classic muscular extension. As your muscles (and connective tissue) become accustomed to this full extension, you find yourself able to achieve and sustain complete relaxation in a position you couldn't even reach a few weeks previously. It should be self-evident that achieving muscular relaxation at increased extension in <u>all</u> your muscles groups will lead to enhanced performance...and in pretty short order, too.

While solo stretching is absolutely convenient and quite effective, sometimes a little help is necessary to achieve full extension. Just as your subconscious mind has to be trained to allow you to run faster, it also has to be convinced that certain muscles can stretch farther than you can do by yourself. A partner who doesn't "feel your pain" can help you stretch beyond your self-imposed limits.

There are two variations on this theme. In the first, the partner increases the amplitude (or range) of your movement simply by pushing you further in the direction you were already bending. In the second, the partner waits until you start to return from your fully extended position and then presses against you as you endeavor to "unbend" from your stretch. The effect here is to teach your muscles to relax when they are in the active unbending stage. By repeating this resistance to unbending over and over, your muscles will become more facile in the transition from work (contraction) to relaxation (extension). In turn, this will increase your range of motion and enhance your overall muscular relaxation.

Free weights are also effective in promoting flexibility (Figs. 35.38-35.41), with the added benefit of simultaneously developing strength. In the same way that your exercise partner increases your range of motion, the influence of the weights causes your muscles to "let go" and extend further than they would under your own efforts. As with the partner-assisted exercises, these free weight exercises increase extension and therefore relaxation.

Fig. 35.38. Bend forward touching the floor with the bar

Fig. 35.39. Legs straight, the bar over the head, bend forward, touching the knees with your forehead

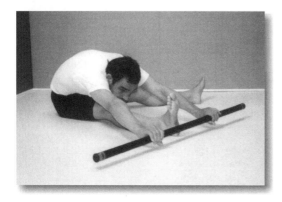

Fig. 35.40. Legs apart, hands on the bar apart, bend with the bar to each foot

Fig. 35.41. Legs apart, hands on the bar together, bend forward touching the floor behind the feet

Swing exercises are yet another way to increase flexibility. Performing leg swings with increasing range of motion and speed once again stretches muscles beyond their normal extension and promotes greater flexibility.

1. Hawk, Steve, Outside Magazine, Volume XXVI, Number 12, December, 2001.
2. Schultz, J.H. 1964, Das Autogene Training, II. Aufl. Stuttgart.

Chapter 36

> *Let me assert my firm belief that the*
> *only thing we have to fear is fear itself.*
> Franklin D. Roosevelt

OVERCOMING THE FEAR OF RUNNING

To get to this point in your development as a Pose Method runner, you've gone through several stages. First you had to accept the simple premise that running was in fact a skill sport that could be learned and improved. You then had to work your way through the various concepts that form the foundation of the Pose Method, accepting them on an intellectual level. From there, you diligently worked your way through the physical process of adopting the new style. And, in this section, you've spent the majority of your time strengthening your body to optimize your ability to make the most of your new style.

In a sense, you're done. You are now equipped to run much better than you ever have before, with a vastly reduced chance of debilitating injury. Any remaining technical errors in your style will be addressed in the final section: Refining Your Running Technique. So...you're free to go. If your objective is to be a happy and healthy recreational runner, skip ahead to the next section, work out any remaining technical glitches in your style and enjoy running as a lifetime sport.

However, if the spirit of competition still lurks in your blood, if PRs and competition still drive you to the start line of road races and triathlons, then you've only just begun. You are still at the start line in your quest to become the best runner you can be. You know the mechanics of running; now its time to become a runner.

Consider again the last sentence of Chapter 18, "The Framing Concept": "All that's left now is to condition your body and mind to go as fast and far as your new running style will let you go." Within that seemingly innocuous sentence are the three pillars of peak performance: technique, endurance and psychology.

While mastering the physical technique of the Pose Method at first seemed perplexing and frustrating and while the strength training for speed and endurance continue to be daunting, the toughest battle will be with your own mind. In this, the final chapter of Section Five, and perhaps most important chapter of the entire book, we deal with the symbiotic relationship among technique, endurance and psychology as they relate to reaching your ultimate performance.

The connection between technique and speed/endurance is relatively straightforward. Perfect technique promotes reduced energy expenditures, smoother, more coordinated muscular movement, muscular relaxation and decreased impact on joints, ligaments and tendons. Conversely, logic dictates that poor technique has the opposite effect: extraneous movements, muscular tension, high impact on joints and connective tissue, all of which lead to wasted energy and increased chanced of injury.

As we settle into a perfect running technique, we further reduce energy use by minimizing "bounce" in our stride and promoting muscular elasticity. By holding to proper framing and not wasting any energy, we create the perfect environment to run as far and as fast as we possibly can. But there are still limitations on our performance. Not surprisingly, those limitations are found within our own minds.

Just as the framing concept of the Pose Method describes a space/time framework within which all the physical aspects of running take place, there is a corresponding mental framework that is vital for your running success. In fact, when the actions of the body are separated from those of the mind, peak performance is impossible. Without the signal from the mind, not even the first step will be taken. And while it is possible to run at a somewhat satisfactory level by training the body and ignoring the mind, you'll find that you may only reach your maximum level of performance by training your mind in lock step with your body.

In keeping with the old aphorism "Mens sana in corpore sano", we have to realize that not only does "a healthy body contain a healthy spirit", but the converse proves the rule, without a healthy spirit, you are unlikely to have a truly healthy body.

Within the context of the mind's involvement in running, we can talk about three levels: the mental, the psychological and the spiritual. Only when all three are truly engaged will you perform the way you've only dreamed you could. Two examples will illustrate what happens when everything comes together for peak performance.

For the first, we recall the oft-told Greek legend of Phidippides. In ancient times, which is to say well before cell phones, pagers, telephones, radios, etc., armies employed trained runners to deliver vital information from location to location. As it happened, according to most versions of the legend, Phidippides was chosen to run a hilly, tortuous course of nearly 140 miles from Marathon to Sparta to request help for the Greeks in their battle with Persia. Phidippides covered the distance in a remarkable two days only to find that the Spartans could not help until the conclusion of a nine-day religious holiday. With that, he reversed his course and ran another 140 miles back to Marathon with the bad news (1).

Realizing that Sparta's help would come too late, the Greek general launched a surprise attack on the Persians and, despite being outnumbered 4-to-1, led his troops to a great victory. With that, the general then dispatched Phidippides to carry news of the Greek victory to Athens.

The Greek success was so grand and the news so overwhelming that, despite his fatigue, he completed the distance, delivered the one word message, "Rejoice," and promptly succumbed. He literally ran himself to death.

But you may not want to die to deliver your best performance. Not to worry. The second example is more universal. In fact, you will probably recognize it your own past, if you have any significant history of running races. Most of the time when running a 5K or a 10K, you will begin to feel bad and, as a consequence, slow down. It basically happens all the time. When hashing over the race with friends, you probably say something like, "I felt like sh-t from 4 miles on."

But every so often, you have a race among races, a race where you set a personal record (PR). And invariably you say to yourself, "That felt really easy. I think I can go a lot faster than that."

Think about it. When you try your hardest, yet suffer and feel bad, you're not running fast, despite all your effort. But when it feels like you're making no effort at all, you're actually running your fastest. That state, where everything is in sync and your fastest performance feels effortless, is the ultimate goal. But achieving that goal, not just once, but routinely, will be the result of a long process of preparation involving physical, mental and ultimately spiritual training. Mastering the mechanics of the Pose Method is just the first stage in a long journey.

As you have progressed through the first chapters of this book, you have been introduced to a system of running that is based on learning certain physical skills that in and of themselves are actually very simple. However, learning them in all likelihood was very difficult. The first step was clearly mental, taking the leap of faith to abandon your previous style and make the commitment to adopt the Pose Method.

That was followed by the first attempts to embrace the Pose technique. In these stages, the physical effort was minimal, but the mental feedback was working overtime. Every time you made an attempt, you were questioning yourself, "did I get it right that time," "is that what I was supposed to do?" All your senses were tuned in, as you questioned whether your foot was landing properly, if you were forcing it back down or just letting it fall, if you were relaxed, tensed, bouncing, driving forward. Simple movements, yes, but so much information for the mind to process.

Mastering the elements of the Pose Method is clearly a much greater challenge mentally than it is physically. After a beginning Pose session, you are not physically exhausted, but you may be mentally drained. And you may be fighting against ingrained habits, thinking that instead of running your normal six miles, you may have covered less than a mile in your Pose Method drills. The urge to "just go out and run" will constantly work at your mind.

At this point you realize that the Pose Method is much more than just a collection of mechanical movements of the legs, arms and body. It is a multi-level phenomenon. Your mastery of the mechanical aspects of the Pose Method will reflect the level of your depth of understanding and the willpower of your personality.

If your mind is open and accepting, determined and focused, you will find it relatively easy to acquire the Pose Method. However if you question the principles and constantly let your mind wander, you will never grasp the basic techniques. The acquisition of these physical skills is basically an exercise in mental control.

The next stage in your development as a runner using the Pose Method comes when you begin to use your new running technique to actually run. At this stage, you're not yet ready to put the mechanics of the run on autopilot – you still need to concentrate heavily on them, in fact – but now you also have to deal with holding perfect running form over longer and longer distances. Again, you may think that this is a purely physical issue, one that is solved by more training, but just the opposite is true.

In almost all cases, runners fatigue mentally, psychologically or spiritually before they reach a true state of physical exhaustion.

Why does this happen? Why do runners "give up" long before they are truly tired? The answer lies in the title of this chapter: "Overcoming the Fear of Running."

Go back to the example where you might say to yourself, "I felt like sh-t from 4 miles on." Why does this happen? The better question is more revealing, "Why did I train myself to make this happen." **Runners habitually underperform because they fear performing better.** They build in their own obstacles and their disappointing performances are really nothing more than self-fulfilling prophecies. Why do you feel like sh-t after four miles? Because you wouldn't have it any other way. That's the bad news. The good news is that just as you have retrained yourself to increase your physical potential with the mechanics of the Pose Method, you can retrain your mind to overcome your self-created obstacles.

Many of us like to use runs as a time to escape daily life, to think through problems, to get away from it all. In other words, when we run, we use our mental energy to deal with issues other than running. While this may be somewhat therapeutic, it won't make you a better runner. Letting life's problems weigh on your mind while you run is equivalent to carrying a 50-pound backpack and loading your arms up with logs. You just can't run faster if you waste either physical or mental energy. If your objective truly is to become a better runner, you must set aside other time to think through your life so that you can approach your runs with a fresh and focused spirit.

Another challenge for a runner is developing the ability to diagnose problems during a run and correct them. Failing to make the correct diagnosis can lead to the wrong "correction" and further erode your performance. A common problem among runners doing long runs is that they believe that fatigue had caused them to shorten their stride. The common diagnosis: increase muscular effort to bring the stride length back to where it was. The immediate result: increased heart rate, increased muscular tension, erosion of form and further diminished performance.

The correct diagnosis is to increase the cadence, taking advantage of muscular elasticity and proper framing. This requires not increased physical effort but greater mental focus to re-direct the body to do what it does best, which is to take advantage of gravity to move forward. Remember, speed is a function of stride length multiplied by cadence. Studies have shown that even elite level runners will see their stride length reduced by as much as 20% during the course of a long race. However, speed can be maintained by increasing turnover. To do so requires conscious control not only to increase tempo but also to fight the temptation to actively attempt to increase stride length.

The foregoing examples of the involvement of mental discipline in the act of running involve conscious decisions and control. Deeper in the psyche, though, we begin to see a point where the conscious mind wages a subtle battle with the subconscious for control of the body. As human beings, we are still very much part of the animal world and have deeply ingrained mechanisms for survival. The very organism of the human body has built-in strategies to avoid danger and protect itself from perceived outside threats.

One such threat can manifest itself in a very long or very hard run. The expended energy and the associated physiological, psychological and mental fatigue associated with a maximum level effort can send a "Danger! Danger!" signal to the organism at the most subconscious level. What started out as a major conscious effort may be perceived by the body as life threatening, something to be halted immediately. Your first response will not be open fear on the part of the conscious mind, but rather physical sensations like muscle stiffness, burning pain, breathing difficulties, intercostal muscle spasms, hammering heart rate, etc.

At this point, in fact, your conscious mind is still giving "full steam ahead" signals, but the subconscious mind, intent on life preservation, begins sending the body a very opposite set of instructions. While the conscious mind may not even "hear" or heed these instructions, often the subconscious takes control of the organism and begins the slowdown process, reducing stride frequency, increasing the time the feet remain on support, increasing muscular tension, leaning the body backwards, landing the lead foot out in front of the body, destroying all form – in short, putting on the brakes in every way possible. And on top of all that, the subconscious fills the body with general discomfort everywhere. The message from the subconscious mind to the body is very succinct: "Slow down – or else!"

Here's the rub of the survival instinct and the opportunity for improvement. In fact, the situation faced by the body and the subconscious is not life threatening, it's just been interpreted that way. And every time the body reached that point and the subconscious mind shut it down, an imprint was made. Over time, the conscious mind developed a whole set of justifications to explain the inevitable slowdown in running pace.

While the subconscious mind initially limits performance, the conscious mind all too often locks in that limited performance as 'just the way it is.' That's why you always feel like sh-t at the four-mile mark, because every time you reach that critical point, you have developed a built-in litany of excuses that are guaranteed to keep you at the same level for years and years.

"I'm not an elite runner, I'm just in it for fun," "I don't need speed work," 'It's too humid today," "This course is just too hilly," and the always reliable "I don't want to peak too soon," – all of these are just examples of the mind's limitless creativity in justifying its own failures. As was mentioned earlier, you train yourself to accept your own limitations. Failure to improve is rarely a physical failure, it's almost always an entirely mental shortcoming.

But there is opportunity here in the interplay between the conscious and subconscious mind. At every level of the human organism, from the cellular, molecular level right up to the complete integrated system called the human being, is an uninterrupted system of checks and balances between the conscious and subconscious mind. Each has its own goals, needs, instincts and satisfaction. And because they seek to fulfill these objectives through the same organism, the relations between the conscious and the subconscious are not always friendly. As one asserts itself, the other must retreat.

In running, for example, the conscious mind may call for a hard session of speed work. The subconscious mind, with its historic duty toward self-preservation, battles that notion by destroying coordination, tensing muscles, ratcheting up the heart rate and burning up vast quantities of energy. This results in an overall slowdown, the direct result of the subconscious mind wresting control from the conscious mind.

This hidden victory by the subconscious mind can guide the conscious mind toward acceptance of inferior performance. As the physical symptoms mount up, the conscious mind has excuses at the ready: "I'm not ready for speed work," "I'm overtrained," " I've already done enough," etc.

More than actual physical readiness, this delicate balance between the conscious and subconscious mind is the reason you have to ease into speed work over a period of time. The goals set by the conscious mind must be believable to the subconscious mind. In order to improve your performance over time, both the conscious and subconscious must buy into the goals and believe they are achievable. If you have been running 400 meter repeats in 75 seconds, you can't just decide to run them in 60 seconds. The subconscious mind will panic and bring that ambition to a screeching halt. However, over the course of 12-16 weeks, you can bring each repeat down a little at a time until you have made the improvement from 75 to 60, that is, if you truly believe.

Of course, there are also the times where the instinct for self-preservation on the part of the subconscious actually overrules the conscious mind and delivers great feats of strength or endurance. Who doubts that we can run faster or jump higher when being chased by a ferocious dog? When the need arises, the subconscious will demand perfect running form and lots of speed, at least until the danger passes.

While such occasions are thankfully rare, they do prove that our physical capabilities are greater than what our conscious mind is prepared to accept. We have it within ourselves to deliver great performances. All we have to do is learn to tap those resources voluntarily.

The next element in our discussion of the relationship of technique, endurance and psychology is a consideration of time. The human body, as a separate entity from the mind, is trapped in the present. But the mind is free to wander back into the past, deal with present issues or ponder future events. As a free agent removed from the same bonds that limit the body, the mind can disassociate itself from the workings of the body, a fact that can play havoc with effectiveness of your running.

While it's nice to think that you can put your body on autopilot and run beautifully while your mind goes on vacation, things rarely work that way. The most common "flight" the mind takes during a long run is toward the future. The body may be at mile six, but the mind begins to calculate what might happen on the way to 26. Instead of monitoring the present performance of the body, the mind starts a whole system of conjecture about how ready the body might be to get through the whole marathon in good shape. By thinking ahead of the present position and of the way to the finish line, the mind is building up a substantial fear of the future, while the physiological and biomechanical process of the body, untended by the conscious mind back at mile six, begin to break down.

When the mind returns to the present from its visit to the future, it finds a physical process in disarray, creating something of a self-fulfilling prophecy. First the mind was concerned about the body's ability to get all the way to the finish line in good form, and then it returns to the present to find things already falling apart long before the finish line even comes into sight.

At this point, it is usually too late to "rescue" a good performance. After all, the signals now coming to the brain from the body are distress signals: the stride has broken down; muscles are sore, etc. The mind, which already had developed a fear of the future, now had those fears confirmed, all because it left the present realm and went off on its own to explore the future.

Clearly, the training of the mind is as essential to successful running as the training of the body. When that training is totally integrated into your overall approach to running, you may hit the zenith and begin to have runs that approach the spiritual realm.

As we discussed earlier, peak performances rarely feel hard. That's because those performances are the result of focused training of both the body and the mind. When you enter that realm, everything feels very natural.

You've probably watched a basketball game when everybody on the court and in the arena realizes that one player is "in the zone," making every shot, no matter from what point on the court. When you're "in the zone", no matter what your sport, you are in a state of super confidence, with total harmony between the body and the mind. Literally every movement is perfect and reflects superb technique and total concentration.

Whether you call it "Zen" or "In the zone", at this point there is no doubt, no hesitation, no mental wandering. The athlete has embraced a specific challenge and has now seized the moment. With a body that is prepared and a mind that is clear and focused, a peak performance is the end result. This is never an accident and it doesn't happen every day.

Peak performances are the result of perfect technique, careful and sustained preparation and complete mental control. From this point forward as you progress in the Pose Method of Running, you must always work on bringing it all together so that you leave fear behind and reach your peak performances right when you most want them.

At its core, fear is a reflection of personal uncertainty. What we do not know, or know very little about, creates an emotional void in our performance, When we try to run while dealing with uncertainty, that void quickly fills with fear...fear of running too hard, fear of not running hard enough, fear of injury, fear of success and fear of failure.

Fortunately, overcoming the fear of running is itself very simple. Fill the void of uncertainty with knowledge. Learn how to run, how to recognize errors and how to correct those errors both while training and racing. Just as with mastering the physical aspects of running technique, overcoming the fear of running is a learning process. Overnight results are not a part of the package.

As you move through the steps to make the Pose Method your 'natural' way of running, you are simultaneously laying the groundwork to overcome your fear of running. Once you have refined your running style, you will have developed a new confidence that will profoundly impact your running performance.

Once you truly understand how to run and have honed your style to take advantage of gravity's unstoppable force, running will seem much easier to you. Rather than view it as a physical exercise in torture, you'll find it to be a very pleasant, stimulating endeavor. You'll find that you don't have to log the miles you once put in, yet you'll be able to run further and faster than ever before.

And, when you know how to run, you'll look at your competitors in a new light, instantly recognizing how few of them truly know how to run. The awareness that you know something your competitors don't is a powerful motivator and creates for you an aura of invincibility. Knowledge plus confidence is the ultimate combination. When you feel like that, you can't wait to run…and run your best.

By merging the mechanics of perfect running technique with a heightened awareness of your physiological and psychological capabilities, you'll elevate yourself to an entirely new level of performance in your running. In a way, it won't even seem like the same sport you either loved or hated for so many years. And you'll be able to run free…free of injury, free of doubt, free of fear.

1. http://www.pbs.org/empires/thegreeks/background/15_p1.html

Section VI

REFINING YOUR RUNNING TECHNIQUE

Chapter 37

The Road to Wisdom?
Well, it's plain
And simple to express.
Err and err, and err, again
but less and less, and less.
Piet Hein

RECOGNIZING & CORRECTING ERRORS

It would be great if you were able to proceed through the first three sections of this book, master the Pose Method of Running and speed off to Olympic Gold, World Records, and Personal Bests or otherwise meet your goals, all without the slightest injury or hesitation. But, as with all physical pursuits learned from a book, there are bound to be glitches along the way. This section of the Pose Method of Running anticipates the errors experienced by most runners and prescribes specific drills to correct them before they cause injury or lead to diminished performance.

Of course, before an error can be corrected, it must first be recognized, then analyzed and understood. What, really, is an error in running technique? An error, by universal definition, is a deviation from the standard or from what is correct. If you follow the prevailing logic that there is no correct running technique, then there is no way to measure a deviation from what is standard or correct, and therefore no way to correct errors.

With the Pose Method of Running, however, we have clearly defined a correct standard of running technique, and therefore have created a means to analyze running style, identify errors and correct them (Fig. 37.1). To summarize, the key elements of the

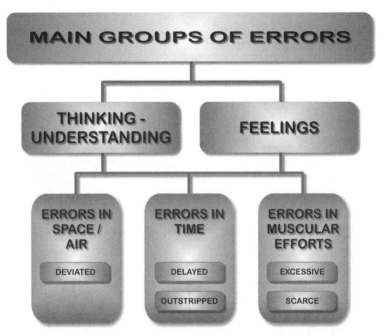

Fig. 37.1. Table of Main Groups of Errors in Running Movements

Pose Method are the following:
1) Use of the Running Pose, with legs bent at all times, the body assuming an "S" - shaped position with support on the balls of the feet;
2) Free falling, with a forward body lean;
3) Using muscular elasticity;
4) Pulling the support foot in a straight line up from the

ground;
5) Using the hamstring to lift the foot;
6) Keeping the body inside the running frame, and
7) Keeping all muscles relaxed.

If all these principles are followed, then the running style will be recognizable by movement where everything is in proportion, where physical effort, acceleration, speed and direction of the various body parts will move in perfect harmony with the trunk of the body. Running correctly, we will never sense any deviation between the physical efforts of our limbs and the general movement of the body (Fig. 37.2).

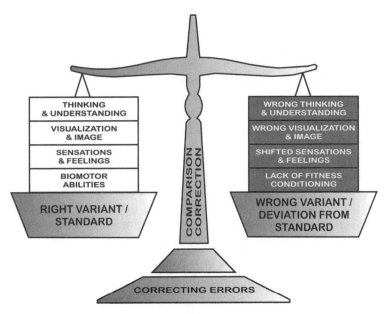

Fig. 37.2. Chart of Correcting of Errors

Conversely, when we run incorrectly, such deviations, while sometimes subtle, stand out. Instead of appearing to be a finely honed machine, the runner appears to be somewhat out of synch. Instead of looking like a single entity moving down the road, the runner like looks like a collection of independently moving parts, erratically lurching forward. It is as if all the musicians in the orchestra are reading the same sheet music, but none of them are following the conductor. All the music is being played, but the sound just isn't right.

Sensing deviations from correct Pose Method running can be a challenge, particularly for runners just adopting the Pose technique. Even if you truly understand the underlying concepts of the Pose Method, interpreting the sensations you feel when you run can be tough. It's a good idea to make it a regular habit to have a training partner or coach observe your running style and compare it with what you are trying to accomplish in the Pose Method.

Any hint of overuse injury should be a signal to recheck your style and correct emerging problems. In your old running style, an overuse injury might have indicated worn-out shoes, but with proper Pose style that is much less likely to be the case. And certain specific injuries will also tell you the cause. If, for example, you begin suffering from shin splints, you can be virtually certain that you are landing with your foot out in front of your body.

Once you have identified an error in your running technique, you must go back to the beginning and make sure that you understand the dynamics of the Pose Method, form the correct visual image of the Pose Method in your mind and correctly interpret the sensations you experience (Fig. 37.3). Only then are you equipped to make the physical changes that will correct the problem.

If you attempt to solve a problem simply by making a physical change in your technique without really working through the underlying concepts and developing a heightened awareness of what perfect running "feels like" the odds are that your problems will reassert themselves once you've made the physical correction and resumed your normal training regimen. Essentially, error correction is not simply a quick fix, but a fundamental restructuring of your total approach to running. Correct a problem from the ground up, and it will stay corrected.

a. Knee and   b. Push off   c. Landing
thigh driving   ahead of the
forward   body

Fig. 37.3. Examples of Visual Errors

Finally, bear in mind that the answer to most problems is simple: "Don't do that!" Invariably, problems are caused by the runner doing too much, exerting too much force, trying too hard. Relax, and let gravity do the work.

Chapter 38

CORRECTING ERRORS IN LEGS' MOVEMENT

The vast majority of running errors come from improper movement of the legs, though there may also be problems with the movements of the trunk and arms. But no matter where the error is pinpointed, there will almost certainly be an accompanying error either in your understanding of the Pose Method or in your interpretation of the sensations you experience when you run. As an example of the latter, go back to the foot tapping drill. It's such a simple exercise, yet when many people perform it they would swear that they are allowing their foot to drop effortlessly to the ground when in fact they are quite actively forcing it down.

That's another reason why it is very helpful to have a training partner not only watch you run, but also watch when you perform the Pose Method drills. If you perform the foot tapping drill incorrectly, but think that you are doing it correctly, then you will proceed through the subsequent drills, and on into Pose running itself, never having developed the knowledge of what Pose running feels like. So, you'll think you are running in the Pose Method, when in reality you aren't.

Your training partner or coach, standing opposite you, can clearly see what you can't when you perform the drill, which is that you *are* pushing your foot down instead of allowing it to fall. And, even if you think you "get" what it feels like from doing just one drill, like foot tapping, you should do all the drills in the sequence. One runner learning the Pose Method was sure he knew what it felt like until he tried the drill where you run in place while changing support from one foot to the next.

While he felt he was doing the drill correctly, his coach finally made it simple, telling him to simply leave his non-support foot where it was (in mid-air) until the other foot got right next to it. What a difference! This was a breakthrough moment as the runner suddenly realized what it felt like to let gravity bring his foot down with no human intervention whatsoever. Ironically, by trying to keep his foot up, he found out how easy it was to let it down.

In both learning the Pose Method and correcting errors (which is really part of the same thing) you can't skip steps. You never know quite when you'll get that "a-ha!" moment and truly understand on a much deeper level what the Pose Method is all about.

Fig. 38.1. Straightened leg

Errors in the movement of your legs fall into three categories: errors where the legs trail the body, where they push out in front of the body and when they interact with the ground.

Legs Lagging Behind The Body

Many things can cause your legs to lag behind your body, all of which fall into the "don't do that!" category. You might simply let your leg stay behind, you might passively straighten

268

it (Fig. 38.1), or kick it behind you aggressively, taking the shin and ankle too high, even past the horizontal (Fig. 38.2).

Of course, it isn't sufficient to simply say "don't do that." You have to go back to basics and remember these key elements of Pose Running:

Fig. 38.2. Overpull behind

1) Begin pulling the support foot from the ground the moment it becomes the support foot;
2) Use only the hamstring to lift the foot from the ground – and stop using the hamstring the moment the contact with the ground is broken;
3) Pull the ankle up under the hip in a straight vertical line;
4) The anterior muscles of your legs (the quadriceps) must remain relaxed and not push the legs forward.

So, to correct the error of the legs lagging behind the body, the emphasis needs to be placed on quickly lifting the foot from contact with the ground while simultaneously letting it bend freely in the knee joint so that it can take a position directly under the hip. To correct this error, we have to focus on proper use of the hamstrings. In fact, virtually all of the drills for learning the Pose Method are oriented to proper use of the hamstrings to lift the support foot from the ground.

In these drills, always bear in mind that what you are training is you own understanding of the feelings and sensations that you should be experiencing when you run. This is not physical training in the sense of increased heart rate and VO2 Max, but sensory training.

Don't look for a "workout" when you do these drills. Instead open your mind and visualize proper technique as you progress from the easier drills to the more difficult ones.

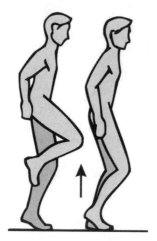

Fig. 38.3. Foot tapping

1) Foot Tapping (Fig.38.3)
Yes, this is the same drill you did earlier, but remember that we're going back to basics here. While you stand in the 'S'-shaped position of the Running Pose, with your weight on one support foot and your knee slightly bent, pull the non-support foot from the ground and allow it to drop back to the ground. Make absolutely certain that the foot drops back down in the same spot every time and that it is right next to the support foot. It is vital to be accurate with your foot placement. After 10-20 reps, switch feet and repeat.

2) Supported Running Pose (Fig. 38.4)
Use chair backs, running hurdles or parallel bars so that you can support your body weight with your arms while your legs are in the Running Pose. Keeping one foot airborne, remove the other from the ground and allow it to drop back to the ground. Again, be precise with the placement of your foot on the ground. Use your hamstring to lift the foot and start every lift as soon your foot touches the ground.

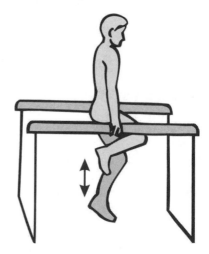

Fig. 38.4. The running pose performed on support on parallel bars

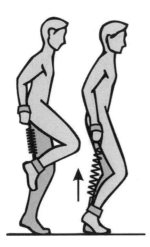

Fig. 38.5. Tapping with the rubber band tied up to the ankles

3) Stretch Cord Tapping (Fig. 38.5)

Affix a loop of surgical tubing around the ankle of one foot, keeping the other end in the hand on the same side. Holding your hand next to your hip, stand with your other foot in the support position in the Running Pose. Tap your non-support foot up and down, using the "rubber band" to help you pull up your foot more quickly each time. The force of the rubber band will give you the sensation of just how quickly it is possible to remove your foot from support. It is this feeling that you need to emulate when you run. Do between 10-20 reps in place on each leg, and then try running with the band on one leg – anything from a rapid 30-100 meters all the way up to a more moderate 800 meters.

4) Partner Running Behind (Fig. 38.6)

Run with your partner running behind you with his hands on your shoulders. Synchronize your leg movements. The effect of having the runner right behind you is to create a frame, limiting the space in which your legs can lag behind your body. Try this for 50-100 meters.

Fig. 38.6. Running with the partner holding hands on shoulders

5) Partner Running In Front, with Stretch Cords (Fig. 38.7)
Now switch positions with your partner and tie a length of surgical
tubing or stretch cord to the same leg on both of you. Your partner,
running in front,
sets the tempo
for the run, which
forces you, in the
trailing position, to
pick up your feet
more quickly to
keep pace. Try this
for distances up to
400 meters. It will
amaze you how
different this feels
than what you had
previously thought
was correct Pose
technique.

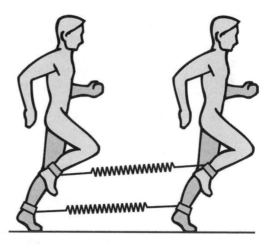

*Fig. 38.7. Running with the partner tied up
with rubber bands in the front*

6) Side by Side Running, with Stretch Cords (Fig. 38.8)

Run side by side with your partner
setting the tempo, your inside legs
attached to the band. Keeping you
strides synchronized, run for up to
400 meters at good pace.

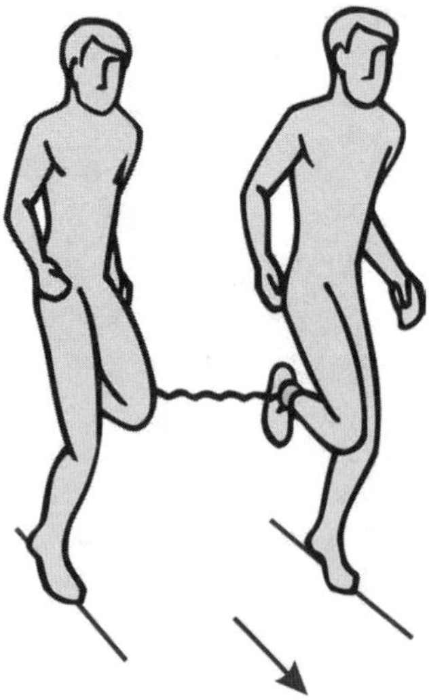

7) Partner Controls Tension (Fig.
38.9)
In this version of running with
surgical tubing, your partner trails
behind you, holding the trailing
end of cords attached to both

*Fig. 38.8. Running side
by side with the partner
tied up with rubber bands*

272

of your legs. As you run, your partner observes your leg action and controls the tension on the bands, "helping" you to a quicker release from the ground. Do this at both slow and fast pace, up to 200 meters.

8) Uphill Running (Fig. 38.10)
Concentrate on pulling your feet up. Don't push off! Keep stride

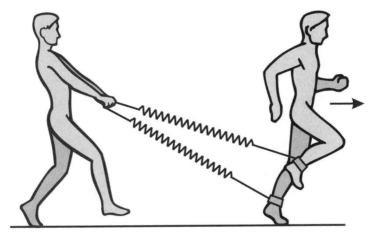

Fig. 38.9. Running with the partner controlling your movements with rubber bands

length short and cadence high and consistent. Start on short slopes and try a variety of lengths and inclines.

9) Stair Running (Fig. 38.11)
We're not talking brutal stadium workouts here. You're doing this as a drill, not training. Just do 10-15, maybe 20 stairs at a time. Keep a steady rhythm as you pick your feet off each stair. Don't push

Fig. 38.10. Running uphill

273

off. Don't put your feet down. Just run through the stairs lightly and rhythmically.

Remember, follow up each of these drills with a short run, perhaps 20-30 meters. The idea is to immediately feel the difference the drills make in your overall running technique. It also helps occasionally to videotape your drills, and then analyze them in slow motion. You will clearly see the difference between correct technique, with your feet coming straight up underneath your body, and incorrect technique, with your feet lagging behind.

Fig. 38.11. Running upstairs

Further improvement in your technique comes from permitting your knee joint to bend freely during the airborne stage. This has the effect of "shortening" your leg, which in turn reduces the pendulum action of the leg in flight. The shorter the swing of the pendulum, the quicker it moves. In addition to increasing quickness, it also reduces any work required to move the leg forward and promotes greater muscular relaxation. Thus, you perform less work and move quickly with reduced muscular tension.

Hamstring Over-Pull

Along the lines of performing less work is another error that can cause your legs to lag behind your body. Over-pull is the problem, and it happens when your hamstrings keep pulling up after your foot has left the ground. The longer you keep pulling up with your hamstring, the further your leg trails your body. As long as it is still being pulled up, it's not free to swing forward. While this isn't terribly common, it can lead to muscular soreness and even injuries.

There are specific drills to address this problem, but first you have to have the proper mental image of the job of the hamstrings. Think of the pistons in your car's engine. They don't perform a long, protracted push or pull movement. They simply "fire" once. The energy released in that single firing is sufficient to propel the piston rod up and do the work of moving the car forward.

Similarly, the moment your foot touches the ground is the "contact" that signals your hamstring to "fire." One quick contraction of the hamstring is all it takes to release your foot from the ground and free the foot to move upward, in a relaxed state, from the momentum of the initial "firing." All the work is done by the hamstring, when the foot actually leaves the ground. The leg is relaxed and moves forward as the result of inertia and momentum.

While many of the previously described exercises address over-pull, there are a few that are very specific to this error.

    1)   Partner Pulling Forward (Fig. 38.12)
For this exercise, your partner is in front of you, controlling the

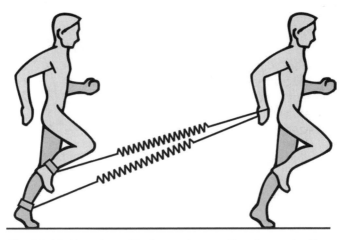

Fig. 38.12. Running with the partner pulling forward with rubber bands

surgical bands attached to your ankles. As he pulls you forward, the tension on the bands prevents your ankle from being brought up behind the hips and past the horizontal. Do this for up to 100 meters, then release the bands and continue running to feel the full effect.

2)   Running In Place, with Stretch Cords (Fig. 38.13)
This time, your partner stands in front of you, controlling the tension on the tubing attached to your ankles. Focus on changing support and maintaining your balance. The objective here, from a "feeling" standpoint, is to try to get your support foot up to where the airborne foot is before the airborne foot falls. Of course, you can't do it, but in the attempt you'll see how automatically the airborne foot relaxes and gently falls to the ground. Do 20-30 reps in one set.

3) Run, with Stretch Cords Overhead (Fig. 38.14)
For this fun variation, you'll want surgical bands that are long enough that you can extend them over your head while they are attached to your ankles. This forces the movement of your feet to go straight up under your hips and emphasizes the first burst of the hamstring. Start with short efforts and work you way up to drills of as much as 100 meters.

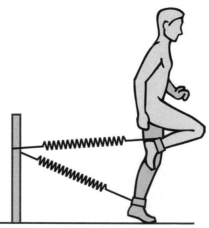

Fig. 38.13. Running in place tied up with rubber bands

Once again, follow each drill with free running. Even better, video tape your running style before doing a set of drills and immediately after, carefully comparing the two to make sure you have eliminated errors. As you evaluate the tape, try to match up

276

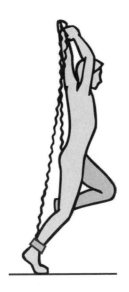

your sense of what you felt while running with the visual images on the tape. Make every effort to imprint the feelings with the images in your mind so that they become the foundation that allows you to run perfectly every time.

Errors in Mid-Air

Once again, errors that occur when the leg is in mid-air tend to be the result of doing too much, not too little. When the swing leg

Fig. 38.14. Running with rubber bands stretched over the head

passes in front of your body, it's because you're either moving your thigh forward and up or moving it forcefully toward the ground. And most likely, you're probably doing both.

This is very understandable, since most of us have always had a mental image of running as being just that: driving forward and pounding the pavement. Now, of course, we know from our intellectual acceptance of the Pose Method that running is something quite different, namely freeing our bodies to move forward under the power of gravity. However, old habits, particularly those as deeply ingrained as a running style, can be very hard to break. So, it's not uncommon at all for runners to truly believe that they are allowing their muscles to relax, when in fact they are still driving forward, expending unnecessary energy and slowing forward progress in the bargain.

Driving the thigh upward is more than just a waste of energy; as it travels upward, it's like a pendulum on the slow, upward half of its swing arc (Fig. 38.15). And while the thigh makes its painfully slow way upwards, the body is now descending toward the ground under the force of gravity. Thus the leg, having been raised too

Fig. 38.15. Excessive upward thigh movement

high, now has to be forced downwards to synchronize its contact with the ground with the descent of the rest of the body. So, in reality, if you drive too hard with your thighs, you will be forced to pound the pavement, and nothing good will come of that. Even worse, the upward drive of the thigh unnecessarily stretches the hamstring, which, having done its work to release the foot from the ground, is supposed to be relaxed at this point. So, in addition to putting tremendous extra stress on your whole body from pounding the pavement, you're making the hamstring work twice as hard as it should.

Correcting the tendency to drive forward with the thighs is done through a series of drills that restrict the forward movement of the swing leg. As with all the other corrective drills, bear in mind that you must first accept the wisdom of restricting this movement, then focus your thoughts on what it "feels like" in the course of the drills.

1) Running Behind Partner (Fig. 38.16)
In this drill, run with your hands on the shoulders of your partner. This limits your ability to push forward with your thighs. In effect, your partner serves as the leading edge of your running frame. Drive with your thighs and you will immediately bang into your

partner, who will not be amused. By having a real barrier at the front of your frame, you are forced to lift your legs vertically. Note the feeling as you run for up to 100 meters behind your partner, then release your hands from his shoulders and continue running exactly the same way.

2) Running With Arms Behind (Fig. 38.17)

A surprisingly effective means of limiting your range of motion is to simply clasp your hands together behind your back and

Fig. 38.16. Running behind the partner with your hands on his soulders

let them hang fully extended. In addition to limiting forward leg drive, this position helps your technique in many other ways. If you

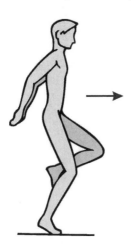

tend to roll your shoulders when you run (another waste of energy) you'll find that impossible with your hands held behind your back. Also, if you've been rolling off your toes instead of lifting your leg from support on the balls of your foot, this will cure that, too. You simply can't "toe off" with your hands behind your back. Use this drill as sort of a "technique check" in the course of a longer run. Intermittently clasp your hands behind your back as you run; if you feel a change in your stride or interaction with the ground, then you've been doing something wrong along the way.

Fig. 38.17. Running with hands held together behind the back

Errors When Landing

It seems so simple, gently placing

your foot on the ground, right under your body. However, the failure to do this can lead to many, many problems for runners. Basically, incorrect interaction with the ground is the source of a great percentage of running injuries. In this category of running errors are overstriding, where the foot strike takes place way in front of the body; landing with the leg straightened (Fig. 38.18); and landing on the heel (Fig. 38.19). Also listed would be active landing, where there is downward force generated by the legs as they approach the ground (Fig.38.20).

Before correcting these errors, you have to truly accept that they *are* errors. Obviously, if you still tend to believe the popularly promoted concept that landing on the heel and rolling through the foot and ultimately toeing off is a proper running technique, well, let's just say you're never going to apply yourself to landing perfectly on the ball of your foot. And you're never going to run using the Pose Method.

Let's think about landing on the heel for a moment. First, it requires that your leg be well out in front of the body. There was a time when we thought this was what running was supposed to be. We used to think that the foot got way out in front of us and then catapulted the body forward. Before we look at that from a technical standpoint, go try a little barefoot run on

Fig. 38.18. Landing with the straight leg ahead of the body

asphalt while landing on your heels. Don't want to do it? Of course not. The pounding would be insane.

If you had no preconceptions and were forced to run across a

Fig. 38.19. Landing on the heel with foot rolling

stretch of asphalt barefooted, you'd automatically find yourself landing on your forefoot, because that minimizes the pounding. Got any doubts? Check out the vintage footage of Ethiopian Abebe Bikila winning the 1960 Olympic Marathon in Rome while running barefoot. Rest assured, he wasn't landing on his heels. And, if you think that's nothing but ancient history, given his winning time (more than 40 years ago) of only 2:15:16, consider that it was easily a world best for the time and consider even further his post race comment that "I could have gone around the course again without any difficulty."

Today's heavily cushioned running shoes mask the pain penalty you pay for incorrect technique, but that doesn't

Fig. 38.20. Active landing with the foot forcefully brought down on support

281

make it proper technique. Landing on the heel lengthens the time you stay glued to the ground (Fig. 38.21), slows your stride frequency, brakes your forward progress, creates a greater load on your joints, ligaments and tendons and removes the free energy provided by gravity from your running equation. All in all, it's a bad bargain, even if it doesn't hurt as much as it should.

To build the proper mental framework for landing on the forefoot, begin with the simple concept that the longer your foot stays on the ground in one place, the greater the braking effect and the slower you move in a forward direction. Not to mention, the less advantage you are taking of gravity's free energy. To get it all right, you want to land with your foot directly under your body as it moves forward in its running frame and you want to make the amount of time that your foot

Fig. 38.21. "Glued to the Ground"

stays in contact with the ground as short as possible. It's really very simple; the less time you spend in any one place, the faster you move down the road.

   1)   The Pony (Fig. 38.22)
The simplest drills always seem to be the toughest to master. Like school figures in ice skating, The Pony is the foundation of proper technique, but in its simplicity lies its challenge: you have to get it absolutely right. Do that and everything else will be pretty easy. When you do the Pony, your objectives are minimal effort, minimal range of motion, no forward progress and perfect balance as you shift your weight from one foot to the other.

Balance with one leg on the ball of the foot and the toe of the other foot barely touching the ground, to allow you to stay balanced. Then quickly shift positions, so that your weight is now on the ball of the other foot and the toe of the previous support foot lightly touches the ground. At first, do these shifts one at a time, with an exaggerated pause in between, making sure that you remain in perfect balance and that your feet are landing directly under your body. Once you get comfortable with the drill, graduate to where you perform the Pony continuously for up to 30 seconds.

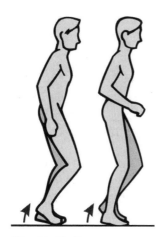

Fig. 38.22. Pony

2)   Cords Around Waist, Tied To Foot (Fig. 38.23)
In this drill (actually a set of drills) a band of surgical tubing is looped around the waist, then draped down the side of one leg, where it is looped around the foot. Actually, you can use a longer band or perhaps use two and attach a loop around each foot. In these drills, the bands act as a guide for the foot; by exerting a direct vertical pull, the feet are left with a path of least resistance that is straight up, and then straight back down. Any attempt to deviate from this pattern is met with increased resistance from the surgical tubing.

With the bands set up in this fashion, you can replicate many of the previously mentioned exercises, from foot tapping and the Pony all the way to running down the trail. With the straight vertical lift assisted by the surgical band, you will find it virtually automatic to have your

Fig. 38.23. Running with the rubber band tied up to the waist

283

foot land exactly where it should, directly underneath your body.

    3)   Barefoot Running on Soft Grass (Fig. 38.24)
Despite the fact that you could run on asphalt, just like Abebe Bikila, it's really not necessary. However, taking a few short trots on soft grass can be really helpful in building the sensory experience of what it feels like to land on your forefoot as opposed to landing on your heel. For this exercise, you can do anything

from a 30-meter trot across a well-maintained lawn to running 18 holes on a lush golf course (after hours, of course).

As you make the transition from heel striking to properly landing on the forefoot, you may experience a temporary period of soreness in the calves. This is not unusual and should not be a cause for concern. This will last for a couple of weeks as your body adjusts to the dynamics of its new running stride, then disappear forever.

Fig. 38.24. Barefoot running on the soft grass

As one runner who learned to run from my previously produced Pose Method of Running video tape said, "after I started to run in the Pose Method, I got temporary soreness in my calf muscles, but the knee and lower back pain are gone…I am going to completely change my running technique to the Pose Method."

    4) Barefoot Running on Soft Sand (Fig. 38.25)
The first cousin of running on grass, sand running has a couple of benefits. First, it's a low tech, but highly effective way to analyze, your running stride. Run 50 meters or so, then backtrack and look at your stride pattern in the sand. If you're still landing on your heels, it will be immediately obvious. Secondly, the longer you stay on "support," the deeper you sink into the sand. If you run

with a light touch and land on your forefoot, you'll skip right over the sand. However, if you land on your heels, you'll become mired in the sand and find that it becomes quite a struggle to make any forward progress.

5) Criss-cross Running (Fig. 38.26)
This previously described drill really reinforces the dynamics on landing on your forefoot. Start by falling to one side and then continue the fall with rapid cross-steps. You won't be able to land on your heels and you won't be able to lengthen your stride. All you can do to go faster is to continue the fall by rapidly changing support from one foot to the next.

Fig. 38.25. Barefoot running on the soft sand

From this point forward in your training, keep in mind the following points about landing: a) land on the balls on your feet, b) make sure your feet land directly under your hips, c) keep your knees bent on landing and d) land softly and easily on the ground, applying no extra force in making contact with the ground.

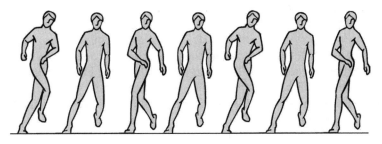

Fig. 38.26. Running sideways with criss-cross leg movement

Correction of Mid-Stance Errors

At first, the concept of mid-stance errors may sound a little unfathomable. After all, the idea of the Pose Method is to be on support for the shortest time possible. How is there even time for an error when you act like the ground you touch is a hot coal? Well, consider the moment when your foot is in momentary contact with the ground to be your checkpoint.

Every time you touch the ground, you should be in the perfect running pose (Fig.38.27). No matter where you are in the course of a given run, if you were to make a video still frame of that instant when your foot touches the ground, it should look exactly the same. But beyond the visual similarities, you should also have the same thoughts and feelings at that moment. You should still be relaxed, balanced, "springy," and compact in your running frame. You should be focused in your mind, with your thoughts focused on channeling of all the efforts of your various body parts into creating a single, efficiently operating biomechanical

Fig. 38.27. Perfect running pose

machine. And you have to constantly be aware of using the minimal amount of energy to produce the maximum results. Most important is to concentrate on the simple matter of shifting your body weight from one leg to the next as subtly as possible, exerting no influence that will slow your forward progress.

The drills to reinforce these concepts are intended to demonstrate the level of fine-tuning necessary to perfect the running pose.

1) Balancing on Medicine Ball (Fig. 38.28)

Seems simple enough. Stand atop a standard medicine ball, in the running pose. While a medicine ball will not easily roll out from underneath you, it will magnify any imbalances in your stance. If you feel an entire cadre of smaller muscles struggling to keep you upright, you'll quickly realize your running pose stance isn't as balanced and light as you thought it was. Master the pose and not only should you be able to maintain the running pose on top of the medicine ball, but you should be very relaxed while you do it.

Fig. 38.28. Balancing on the medicine ball

2) Hops in Running Pose (Fig. 38.29)

Again, the emphasis is on maintaining balance and relaxation as you perform very light-touch hops, both in place and with minimal forward progress. The idea is not to bound over some large object, but instead to use minimal energy and your muscular elasticity to quickly contract your hamstring and remove your foot from support for an instant.

3) Jump Rope Exercises (Fig. 38.30)

Perhaps the perfect exercise to demonstrate the application of the minimal amount energy necessary. The concept in jumping rope is to leave just enough space for the rope to pass under the feet. You don't jump high; you just change support and use your natural springiness to create the necessary clearance. Even better, you automatically land on the balls of your feet, never on your heels.

It's a good idea to video tape all three of these drills, checking (in slow motion) for the number of frames between the mid-stance and the landing positions. The quicker you make transition from mid-stance to the running pose, the faster you will run. The whole cycle of movement depends on an earlier start to the forward-falling movement and a quicker foot release, which leads to a

287

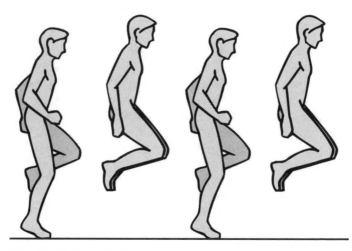

Fig. 38.29. Hops in the running pose

higher stride frequency and a greater use of gravity's pulling effect.

In all these drills, even if you're working with the medicine ball and jump rope in a gym, always do a short run after each exercise, concentrating on emulating the feelings you derived from each drill into your actual running technique. Always stay in the running pose, but change quickly and effortlessly from one leg to the other.

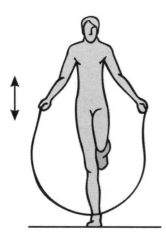

Fig. 38.30. Jumps with the rope

Errors in "Take-Off"

Interesting, isn't it, that the take-off phase is saved for last? In most running instruction, "take-off" gets the lion's share of the attention and words like "push" and "drive" are used to emphasize the importance

288

of propelling yourself forward. By now you should be able to anticipate my own advice: don't do it. Don't take-off. Don't propel yourself forward. Don't pay any attention to it.

No, I don't propose canceling any laws of physics or classic mechanics. I'm not suggesting that Sir Isaac Newton was wrong. We're all on the same side here. What I do suggest is that you look at this phase of running technique in a new light.

Instead of thinking that you must do the work to move yourself forward, think about which force is greater and more immutable: your personal strength or the force of gravity. To put this in context, think about running down a steep hill. Any experienced runner knows that the problem here is not running fast, but running *too* fast. More often than not, your concern is how to control the speed, not unleash it.

The entire concept of the Pose Method of Running is to free gravity to be just that effective on flat land. Remove support from under your body and gravity is free to do its work, exactly as if you were pointed straight down hill. And anything you do to counteract gravity will only slow you down. Inherent in the concept of "take-off" is work performed against gravity. When you push off from the ground, you're actually fighting gravity, not freeing it to do its work. So don't do it.

Don't straighten your legs. Don't toe off from the ground. Don't push (Fig. 38.31).

Here's an analogy of how it works on flat ground. Imagine being connected to a motorbike with one of your surgical tubes (Fig. 38.32).

Fig. 38.31. "Don't push"

289

The bike has the power to generate speeds such as you would experience when running downhill. If you tried to keep up by straightening your legs and toeing off, you would soon find yourself bounding along, absorbing great punishment throughout your entire skeletal system, before you fell flat on your face. But if you could manage to simply get your legs out of the way, changing support quickly, you could go much faster and stay upright. Substitute gravity for the power of the motorbike and you've got the concept. Your job is to stay relaxed and let gravity take over. That's the Pose Method of Running.

What drills are appropriate for this? All of them! Everything you have done to this point is designed to help you maintain a relaxed, supple stance while getting your feet out of the way and freeing gravity to move you forward. Nothing could be easier.

Fig. 38.32. Running behind the motorbike

Chapter 39

CORRECTING ERRORS IN TRUNK MOVEMENT

What is the function of the trunk of your body in running? Does it move? Does it contribute to forward progress? Is it active or passive? Is it carried or does it do the carrying?

Essentially, your trunk is the container for your body mass (Fig. 39.1). It must be strong, to carry all your weight in proper posture without fatiguing. It must be resilient, to minimize any shock. And it must be "quiet", to prevent any unnecessary movements that would detract from smooth forward progress.

While it seems a simple

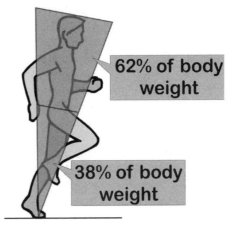

62% of body weight

38% of body weight

Fig. 39.1. Body weight distribution. The heavier top of the body allows for the easier fall forward out of balance

291

matter to say that you must maintain a relaxed upright carriage to your body, there are a number of subtle deviations that can intrude upon your technique and make your running far less effective.

The first of these is bending the trunk forward, which might be caused by fatigue or which you might do thinking that you are leaning forward to free up the pull of gravity (Fig. 39.2). In the Pose Method, a forward lean is with the whole body; it is not folding the upper body forward from the waist.

If you bend the trunk forward, you automatically increase tension in your back muscles. You also begin pushing your legs forward, in a protective

Fig. 39.2. Bending the trunk forward is not leaning forward

psychological reaction to prevent a fall. The forward push of the legs not only wastes energy, but it also creates a braking effect. So, merely by bending forward at the trunk, you've increased muscular tension while working harder and running slower. Bad plan.

Just as bad a plan is deviating your trunk backwards (Fig. 39.3). You might do this because of a psychological reaction to fatigue and speed. Thinking that you're going a bit too fast for your current condition, you lean backwards to subconsciously

Fig. 39.3. Deviating the trunk backward is actually stopping the forward movement of the body

292

apply the brakes. But instead of allowing you to rest, this reaction makes it harder to move forward. Your legs sneak back out in front of your body, you minimize the chance for gravity to draw you along, and your biomechanical efficiency is totally compromised.

A less common error is the tendency of the trunk to swing sideways, probably caused by excessive weight transfer from one leg to the next (Fig. 39.4). The likely culprit is the desire to push forward. This active force of the legs gets the trunk moving and the resulting oscillation actually limits the legs' free motion, making it tougher to leave support.

Finally, your shoulders may become too active, rolling from side to side. The shoulders do not contribute to forward progress; their rotation only reflects what is happening with the legs. If you run properly, your shoulders will remain "quiet," with minimal rotation in time with the change of support. If, however, your stride deviates from the vertical line, that in turn can increase the rotation of your shoulders. Which, in turn, serves to further magnify, the deviation of your legs. In short, the wheels come off and a once efficient stride becomes exaggerated and inefficient.

Fig. 39.4. The trunk swing sideways creates unnecessary oscillation of the body

The key to correcting these errors of your trunk is first to think through the Pose Method and remind yourself of the role of the trunk, which is to keep your body mass in check while your hamstrings do the work of switching support from one leg to the next.

One of the simplest ways to check for a quiet trunk is to run with your hands in clenched fists, extended straight out in front of you and held side-by-side (Fig. 39.5). If you notice your hands deviating significantly to the left or right, you can be sure that

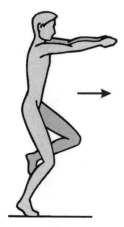

Fig. 39.5. Running with the arms in front, hands held together

you are driving with your legs, essentially trying too hard. Try the same drill with your hands held behind you and you'll get a good feel for the elasticity of your hip and leg action (Fig. 39.6). You can even watch your shadow when you run, looking for signs of excessive motion or bad posture in your running style. And always concentrate on the fact that the work is being done underneath the trunk, not by the trunk. Just like the chassis of a car is transported by the movement of the wheels and contributes nothing to its forward progress, the trunk of your body is just along for the ride and should do nothing to hinder – or help – your smooth progress down the road.

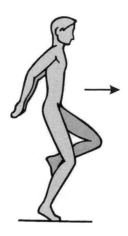

Fig. 39.6. Running with the hands held behind

Chapter 40

CORRECTING ERRORS IN ARMS' MOVEMENT

What do we consider an error in the movement of your arms while you run? At its most basic level, you are making a mistake if your arms are not working in perfect synchronized coordination with your legs. When we run, we act as a complete, balanced, integrated mechanical unit. The movement of the legs is the deciding factor in how the rest of the body performs; any work not synchronized with the movement of the legs will literally throw the runner out of whack.

Keeping the work of the arms balanced with the demands of the legs is largely a mental process, one that harkens back to many of our preconceived notions about running performance. Just as we create problems when we attempt to "drive" forward with our quads when the legs are in the air, any attempt to propel ourselves through active driving with the arms inevitably leads to a breakdown of the perfect running style we are trying so hard to maintain.

The best example of this probably comes in an attempt to make a 100% effort sprint at the end of a mile or 5K. Desperate to wrest the last full measure of speed from a fatigued body, the runner turns to the arms for some extra "juice" (Fig. 40.1). The arms begin

295

swinging harder...and what happens? First, the over-swing of the arms causes a deviation from the carefully charted straight-ahead line toward the finish. Second, urgently needed energy is channeled from the legs, which need everything they can get, to the arms, which are now taking up more than they need. Third, in a reaction to the sudden upturn in energy, the arms receive a massive injection of lactic acid, turning them to stone in a matter of seconds. The resulting pain sends a most unpleasant message to the brain, something along the lines of "all systems shutting down – now!"

Fig. 40.1. "Active arms' work." Unnecessary muscles' activity of the arms does not contribute to forward movement of the body

What happened to our game, but foolish, runner was a complete loss of balance. In the first instance, the over-swing led to a loss of physical balance. The excessive movement of the arms has destroyed the physical balance, adding rotation to the hips and making the whole body struggle to stay upright and moving in the straightest possible line toward the finish.

Second, the critical balance of the body's energy reserves was compromised, just when they were needed most. Instead of being able to channel every last bit of energy to the legs, the body was not only forced to send huge amounts to the arms, but also had to divert extra energy to other parts of the body as they made their best efforts to maintain the straight ahead course.

And finally, all this disruption of technique, and the resulting pain, ruined the most critical aspect of our runner's performance, mental balance. Instead of a quiet body allowing a quiet mind to finish the job, the over-exertion of the arms has rendered the mind a confused place, dealing with all kinds of terrible information and pain, resulting in a loss of focus and a flood of negative thoughts.

You've probably seen this situation even in the Olympics, when a runner seems to lose all coordination approaching the finish line. Instead of flowing smoothly toward the line, the approach to the line is spasmodic, jerky, completely out of control. The crowd enthusiastically applauds the guts and determination of the athlete, but the reality is that by trying too hard, and doing the wrong things, the runner's performance falls to pieces. It's not a pretty picture.

So, it's very tempting for the runner to want to do everything possible to achieve the best possible performance, but as with so many things in the Pose Method, doing everything possible really means doing exactly the right things, as well as avoiding doing the wrong things. You must have the proper mentality and grasp of the technique to perform your best when it is most important.

Let's go back to the notion of the runner as a mechanical system. As we know, the legs do the real work, making the rest of the body subordinate. In this mechanical system, there is an inherent and consistent flow of energy from the legs, through the trunk and out into the arms. This flow, or transformation, of energy is significant in the physical balance of the body, and the arms play a vital role in maintaining this balance (Fig. 40.2).

Basically, the more balanced the body is, the straighter trajectory the body maintains in its forward progress down the road. In other words, the greater the level of balance, the greater the level of mechanical efficiency. As the body operates at peak mechanical efficiency, there is a reduction in the overall energy needed to sustain movement and a significant reduction in the mechanical load placed on the body, meaning, in plain English, that smooth balanced running is easy on the bones, the joints, the tendons, the ligaments and the muscles.

In the mechanical progression of running, the action starts with

Fig. 40.2. "Arms' Balance."
Arms play a balancing role in the body movement

the act of falling forward, followed immediately by the rapid change of support from one leg to the next. As an automatic reaction to maintain balance, the body "adds" a slight rotation of the shoulders, which takes place on the opposite side of the leg being removed from support, thus helping maintain balance. As the shoulders rotate, there is a corresponding movement of the arms.

In this sequence of movements, the arms are basically at the end of the line; their movement should be the minimum possible to maintain perfect balance. As this sequence of movements takes place, the energy flows along the same route. The free and unrestricted movement of energy along this pathway leads to freedom of movement of the whole body and all its parts, which releases any excess tension in the muscles. The role of the arms, then, is to "listen" to the legs and body and be ready to react to any changes in their activity, by making the necessary adjustments to maintain balance

For example, if you stumble on a rough trail, the arms instantly make the adjustments to correct balance and assist you as you return to optimal form as soon as possible. Unless called upon in such a situation, the arms are always at the ready, doing as little as possible to maintain perfect form and balance.

This means specifically that you don't put them to work by

exaggerated pumping, trying to speed them up to move faster than your legs, swinging them in front of your body or up to your shoulders. Don't do any of that. Keep the carriage of your arms free and easy, relaxed, moving minimally, synchronized with the legs and ready to react in an instant if needed.

Chapter 41

*God sells all things
at the price of labor.*
Leonardo da Vinci

RETAINING THE POSE TECHNIQUE
IN YOUR TRAINING

In today's culture of immediate gratification, there is an expectation that anything desired can be attained. Whether you want to "Lose Weight Now" or start to "Earn Six Figures", there's always someone out there who promises to deliver what you want, usually in six weeks at a cost of only three easy payments.

Common sense, however, dictates a more reasonable approach. You can desire virtually anything reasonable, but the cost usually involves extreme dedication, hard work and an unwavering commitment to your goals. And that is why so many people fail to attain the things they most covet. Once they find out how difficult it is to stay committed to a goal over a long period of time, they usually decide they can do without whatever it is they thought they wanted. If all the best things in life came so easily, then they really wouldn't have value and everybody would have them.

The reality is that most overweight people remain that way and most low-income people stay in the lower tax brackets, not because they lack the ability to control their destiny, but because they lack the commitment to follow through with a sensible program that will bring them what they desire. Learning a physical skill such as the Pose Method of Running is no different. You may grasp the basic elements of the technique on your very first try, but fully integrating the Pose Method into your battery of physical and mental skills is a lifetime process.

Without a doubt, you will reach a point during the process of learning the Pose Method when you inevitably ask yourself how you can maintain the Pose Method over the course of a long run. By this time, you've "got" the idea and can complete a short run in admirable Pose fashion, but find that when the distance increases your mind wanders and your form falters.

This is actually no different than the situations described above when people fail to follow through on their ambitions: their minds wander. At first, people dedicated to a new goal are very focused on the task at hand, but without fail, life intercedes. A "born again" dieter, caught up in the pace of life, finds it easier to turn into the fast-food drive-through and winds up eating fatty foods; a newly devoted investor splurges on a new car and upends a well-conceived money management plan. It happens all the time.

The same thing happens on an individual run, as well as on a perfectly planned running/learning program. On any given run, particularly during the initial learning phase, you start out fresh, focused and motivated. Trying to grasp the intricacies of this new Pose Method technique, you concentrate all your thoughts on your technique. But as the run progresses, your mind moves on to concerns like crossing the street safely, reacting to the approach of a nasty looking dog or maintaining a certain pace. While all that moves to the forefront, you suddenly start thinking about a situation at work that you want to think through or perhaps plans for the weekend that need to be finalized. Then fatigue creeps in.

Now your mind, which was so focused on pure technique at the beginning of the run, is dealing with a half dozen or more issues.

302

The result will be a deterioration of the very form you were trying so diligently to master. Even if you're not terribly tired, your best option is to stop running, either to take a pause and regroup your thoughts or to just call it quits for the day. The important thing is to run only when you can focus your mind on the act of running. If you continue to run once your form has deteriorated, you will be training yourself to run poorly.

Similar distractions or lack of attention can creep into your program over the long haul. When you first embark on the mission to learn the Pose Method of Running, you are no doubt eager to improve your running and reap the benefits of improved technique. But over time your enthusiasm for the learning process will wane and you will want to enjoy just going out for a run and not thinking about it. Or you may have keyed into just a couple of elements of the Pose Method with which you feel comfortable. "If I keep my legs bent, stay within my frame and don't pound the pavement," you say to yourself, that's all I need to do to run properly.

While keying into those particular elements is a good thing and will help you run injury-free for years and years, it means only that you are running properly, but not running well. You've keyed in on form, but relaxed on function. Basically, by ignoring the equally important factors of rapid cadence and minimal time spent on support, you've entered a comfort zone that means you will no longer improve. You've hit a plateau and you will stay there.

Interestingly, when you look at all the factors that can impede your progress in completing longer and/or faster runs using the Pose Method, you notice that pure physical fatigue is probably the least important. Great running, like excellence in golf, gymnastics or ballet is really a physical manifestation of extremely strong mental ability. When you hit the plateau where your times remain the same, you haven't reached a physical limit; you've made a conscious decision not to run any faster. Each time you go out for a run, you say to yourself something like "I won't push it today." There it is. Decision made. Progress stopped.

There is considerable irony in this. From a purely mechanical standpoint, the Pose Method of Running has been conceived to be simplicity itself. As indicated by the St. Exupery quote at the beginning of the "Do Nothing" chapter, everything extraneous has been removed from the Pose Method and what is left is utterly necessary to forward locomotion.

Yet, by stripping away all of the excess and wasted energy in reducing the act of running to its elemental form, we have increased the dependence on mental strength. The technique of the Pose Method is more than just the mechanics of running; it is an integrated approach that demands utter concentration.

In your early efforts to master the mechanics, it was enough of an accomplishment to run 25 or 30 yards correctly in the Pose Method. Then, as the Pose Method began to feel more natural to you, you could up the distances to where you were running two or three miles while remaining in correct form.

Yet, it wasn't an easy task to maintain proper technique as the length of your runs grew greater. Being accustomed to the effects of fatigue, you lost concentration on your movements, as if poor form was the inevitable result of physical fatigue. The reverse is really true: maintaining good form will help delay physical fatigue and improve your overall performance. And the ability to maintain that form is the result of mental and psychological conditioning.

The process of learning the Pose Method is a lifelong journey, starting with the elemental mastery of simple physical movements and proceeding to complex psychological strength. There are no vacations from this process, only constant learning and control. Every run is a new chance to bring greater depth to your new skills; every race is an exploration of your physical and mental capabilities.

Over time, you will cease to think of what you are doing as the Pose Method of Running. Instead, you will regard it as running, pure and simple. And that's all it is, running as simple as nature intended and as complex as the human mind can comprehend. That is when you will be able to maintain the Pose Method, not just for the long run, but for a lifetime.

ABOUT THE AUTHORS

Dr. Nicholas S. Romanov was born and educated in Russia. After graduating with honors from the faculty of Physical Education of Chuvash State Pedagogical University and spending one year in Soviet Army service, he continued his professional career at Chuvash Pedagogical University as a lecturer in theory and practice of track and field and as a coach for the University track and field team. At the same time, he studied at the All-Union Scientific Research Institute of Physical Culture in Moscow in the laboratory of the renowned Soviet Union sport scientist and coach, Professor Vladimir M. Diachkov.

After receiving his Ph.D. in Physical Education from Russian Academy of Physical Culture and Sports in Moscow, Dr. Romanov advanced to become the Head of the Department of Sport Disciplines, Head Track and Field Coach, and senior lecturer of Sport Biomechanics, Theory and Practice of Physical Education and Sport Training, Theory and Practice of Track and Field. In the mid-70s, he developed the Pose Method, which enhances efficiency and performance in running, track and field, swimming, cycling, gymnastics, speed skating, and cross-country skiing.

In 1993 Dr. Romanov moved to Miami, Florida and founded his own workshop, using the Pose Method to train triathlon and running technique to elite, age group and recreational athletes from the United States, Latin America, Canada, Europe, South Africa and Australia. In 1997 he released his first educational video "The Pose Method of Running", which continues to sell around the World, helping runners and triathletes improve their performance and dramatically reduce injuries, allowing numerous athletes to return to training and racing after injuries.

Dr. Romanov currently conducts clinics and seminars in the USA, Mexico, England, and South Africa in association with sports clubs, national governing bodies, and universities. He served as a member of the USA Triathlon coaching committee from 1996-2002, as a consultant for British Triathlon in 2000 Olympics in Sydney, and as a coach of British triathletes since 2001.

Scientific research supporting the Pose Method has been conducted at the USA Olympic Training Center in Colorado Springs (G. Dallam, 1998), Florida Atlantic University (C. Sol, 1999), Sheffield Hallam University, UK (G. Fletcher. 2001), Cape Town University, South Africa (T. Noakes, 2002), and Kubansky State University, Russia (A. Pianzin, 2003).

At 51, Dr. Romanov resides with his wife, Dr. Svetlana Romanov, and their three children, in Miami.

Co-author John Robson resides a brisk four-minute run from the azure waters of the Atlantic Ocean in Miami Beach, Florida.  At 51, he takes frequent jaunts, with wife Gay and daughter Jane, to Costa Rica, Mexico, North Carolina, California and, lately, Hawaii to indulge his dual passions for surfing and cycling. Closer to home, trail running, skateboarding and swimming serve as palliatives for the almost criminal lack of waves in those aforementioned azure waters.

He continues as a frequent contributor to Florida Sports Magazine and the Miami Herald. Over the years, he has written for a wide variety of publications and online sites including Active.com, Gorp.com (the Great Outdoor Recreation Pages), MountainZone.com, the New York Daily News, Outside Magazine (less than 300 words in one shining contribution), Billboard Magazine and Music*Sound OUTPUT.

A 1973 graduate of Washington & Jefferson College, he is a former executive with a prominent international interactive music television network, has for the last seven years been partnered in a music marketing firm and now carries a business card identifying him as *Heavy Lifter* for the start-up label Hydrogen Records.

Appendix A

Definitions

General Center of Mass (GCM) of the body - point in a body or system of bodies which moves as though it bore the entire mass of the body or system. Point around which the mass and weight of a body are balanced in all directions.

Ground Reaction Forces (GRF) – Newtonian principle, where every force is met with an equal and an opposite force. The force with which foot hits the ground is met with an equal force that exerted by ground to the foot, and can measure up to 3-4 times body weight.

Muscle Elasticity - muscle's ability to quickly return to normal length after being stretch under some loading and quickly released from it.

Range of Motion (ROM) – area covered by a limb or body during movement.

Ball of the foot (BOF) – also referred to as the forefoot in running literature, the area under the sesamoid joint, 1-st metatarsal and big toe.

Pose Concepts

Pose – Most important position in running from which all movement is generated.

Wheel – Reproduction in running of three major mechanical properties of the wheel - constant position of the general center of mass (GCM) above the support point, constant position of GCM on the same height without vertical oscillation and constant change of support. Application of it to running happens by keeping GCM of the body above the forefoot on the ground, reducing vertical oscillation of the body during change of support and keeping change of support very short.

S-spring Stance – Keeping the runner's body perfectly balanced on one leg, with weight above the forefoot and knee bent, making the body compact and loaded with elastic energy.

Change of Support (CS) – Shifting the body weight from one leg to the other.

Vertical Action – Pulling the support foot from the ground up under the hip.

Gratuitous Forces – Gravity, elasticity, inertia, Coriolis – forces working without the ATP breakdown.

Rules of Good Running Technique

1. Keep your body as a whole leaning forward from your ankles and free falling.
2. Keep shoulders, hips and ankles along one vertical line.
3. Always keep your knees bent, don't straighten them.
4. Keep your support and body weight on balls of your feet (forefoot).
5. Change support quickly from one foot to the other.
6. Pull the ankle from the ground straight up under the hip by using hamstring muscles during change of support.
7. Make your support time short.
8. Retain your support easy, effortlessly, light.
9. Don't push off or toe off, lift only.
10. Don't land on the heels or put weight on them while on support, they can only slightly touch the ground.
11. When on support, keep your feet behind the vertical line going through the knees and hips.
12. Don't move your weight to toes; pull your ankle up when weight is on the balls of the feet.
13. Don't try to increase your stride length or range of motion to increase your speed, they are function of speed.
14. Don't move your knees and thighs too far apart, forward and backward during the stride.
15. Don't move ankles back and forth, only up and down.
16. Keep knees and thighs hanging down and relaxed during swing.
17. Don't fix on landing, just lifting.
18. Your legs should land themselves without any muscle activity, just by gravity pull, stretch reflex and momentum.
19. Don't point toes and don't land on them.
20. Keep your ankles in a neutral position without pointing or dorsoflexion.
21. Arms' performance is a natural balance for legs' movement.

Running Technique Principles Reminder

1. Integrate the movements in running through the POSE.

2. The main pulling and integrating force for this is GRAVITY.

3. Freedom of running means FREE FALLING.

4. The use of muscle force is actually the skill of ASSISTING GRAVITY.

5. The movement of the body in free falling is secured through constantly destroying the balance and BREAKING CONTACT WITH THE GROUND.

6. Breaking contact with the ground is actually achieved through pulling the support foot vertically up UNDER THE HIP.

7. Pulling the support foot is done by the hamstring muscle in THE RUNNING POSE.

8. Adhere to PULLING, NOT PUSHING, philosophy.

9. Running is the SKILL OF MOVEMENT.

10. Technique is a channel for USING AND SHARPENING psychological and physiological abilities.

Appendix B

Common Errors in Running

The errors are defined as: deviation from the standard.

A. Pain

> • Pain comes from only one reason - you are doing something wrong. It is a warning that something is happening or is about to happen, while you are interacting with support (and through it with gravity).

B. List of Errors

> 1. Landing with the HEEL FIRST
>
> 2. HEEL STRIKE with a straight leg
>
> 3. Landing ahead of the body - OVERSTRIDING
>
> 4. Using quad muscles instead of the hamstring (PUSH OFF); pulling the swing thigh and knee forward and up
>
> 5. Landing on the toes with the BODY BEHIND landing (General Center of Mass behind foot)
>
> 6. Landing with STIFF LEG/ankle
>
> 7. "ACTIVE" LANDING
>
> 8. OVERALL MUSCLES TENSION
>
> 9. ACTIVE PUSH-TOE OFF, straightening the leg to propel the body forward
>
> 10. Holding the REAR LEG BEHIND after leaving the support
>
> 11. LEANING THE TRUNK sideways, forward
>
> 12. Keeping SHOULDERS UP AND STIFF
>
> 13. ARMS "PUMPING"
>
> 14. WRONG THINKING (commands to yourself)
>
> 15. WRONG IMAGE (visualization)
>
> 16. WRONG FEELINGS (on muscles' tension/relaxation)

C. How to identify them (by common related injuries)

1 Landing heel first (heel striking) / straightening the leg

• Knee pain (Patello-femoral)

• Hip pain

• Lower back pain

2 Landing in front or ahead of knee joint

• Stress fractures

• Shin splints

3 Using quad muscles

• Muscles soreness

• Heel striking leading to eventual knee pain

• Hamstring injury

4 Landing on toes (high heels)

- Shin splints
- Plantar fasciitis
- Achilles tendonitis
- Calf muscle soreness

5 Landing with stiff leg/ankle

- Plantar fasciitis
- Achilles tendonitis

6 Active landing

- Stiff ankle/leg (muscle tension)
- Plantar fasciitis
- Achilles tendonitis

Appendix C

Recommended Reading

Alexander R.M., Elastic Mechanisms in Animal Movement, Cambridge University Press, Cambridge, 1988

Alexander R.M., The Human Machine, Columbia University Press, 1992

Aristotle, The Complete Works of Aristotle, Revised Oxford Translation. Edited by Jonathan Barnes, Volume one, Bollingen Series LXXI-2, Princeton University Press, 1984; Movement of Animals, pp. 1087-1096, Progression of Animals, pp. 1097-1110,

Biomechanics of Distance Running, editor Peter R. Cavanagh, Human Kinetics Books, Champaign, IL, 1990, pp. 362

Brown, T. Graham, Note Upon Some Dynamic Principles Involved in Progression. The British Medical Journal, September, 1912, pp. 785-787

Dilman, C. J., Kinematic Analysis of Running. Exercise and Sport Sciences Reviews., Vol III, 1975, pp.193-218

Doherty, J.K., Modern Track and Field, Prentice-Hall, 1963. Running Style on Middle and Distance Running.

Dyson, G.H.G, Running.The Mechanics of Athletics, University of London Press, Ltd., 1967, pp. 109-124,

Fenn, W.O., Work Against Gravity and Work Due to the Velocity Changes in Running. American Journal of Physiology, Volume 93, pp. 433-462

Hay, J. G., Track and Field: Running. The biomechanics of Sports Techniques. Press-Hall, Inc., 1986, pp. 395-414

Housden, E.F., "Mechanical analysis of the Running Movement," in 'Run, Run, Run., Ed. by Fred Wiet, Los Altos, California, Track & Field News, Inc., 1964, pp. 240-245

Margaria, R., Biomechanics and Energetics of Muscular Exercises, Oxford University Press, London, 1976

Newton, A. F. H., Running, H.F. & J Witherby, London, 1935, pp. 21-22, 36.

Robbins, S.E. & Jouw, G.J., Athletic Footwear: Unsafe due to Perceptual Illusions. Med. Sci. Sports Exercise Volume 23, 1991, pp. 217-224